IN & AROUND
LONDON

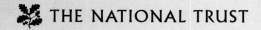
THE NATIONAL TRUST

WALKS
In & Around London

Peter Wenham

First published in Great Britain in 2003 by
National Trust Enterprises Ltd
36 Queen Anne's Gate, London SW1H 9AS

www.nationaltrust.org.uk

Cataloguing in Publication Data is available from
the British Library

ISBN 0 7078 0319 5

Series Editor Liz Dittner
Designed by David Stanley
Typesetting & Origination by GS Typesetting
Maps by Malcolm Porter
Printed by Wing King Tong Co Ltd, Hong Kong

National Trust Walks: In and Around London
published in 2003 by National Trust Enterprises Ltd

KEY TO SYMBOLS

| Historic building | Industrial heritage | Wheelchair Access |

| Association with famous painter | Literary connections | View |

| Coniferous woodland | Broadleaved woodland | Flora |

| Film Associations | Refreshments | Fauna |

CONTENTS

INTRODUCTION

For some fifteen years I accompanied my wife around a great number of National Trust properties as she sought to improve facilities for disabled visitors. Due to time constraints and because the major difficulties of access were often within the houses we visited, we did very little walking. When we did, it was with wardens who had taken steps to upgrade paths, lessen obstacles etc. In most cases the walks were short and easy. So, although always enjoyable as a break from driving an average of 30,000 miles a year to and from Trust properties, I had almost forgotten the pleasures of walking distances in excess of a mile. This year we began a voyage of re-discovery.

I took a decision, at the outset, to try to include at least one Trust property in every walk even though some, as I mention in the book, are places likely to be known only to those who keep Properties of the National Trust as bedtime reading!

Before continuing, I want to place on record my belief that in its wardens and country managers the National Trust has a superb, irreplaceable, resource. Whenever I meet them my faith in the Trust is strengthened, for they understand the bond between land and people, and are, very often, the public face of the Trust, even if that simply includes chatting to dog-walkers on wet winter mornings. Without the unstinting help of the wardens, this book would hardly have been possible and would certainly have been infinitely less pleasurable to write.

What follows is a brief survey of what you can, I hope, discover when taking these walks.

The Wandle is a remarkable river, full of industrial history and, in recent years, an example of what can be done by determined enthusiasts to reclaim an urban wasteland. When I first knew it the river resembled a sewer; today there are trout in the upper reaches and, sitting in my office (shed!) beside it, I often see kingfishers flashing past. There are problem areas, far outweighed by

Right: Peacock topiary in the Long Garden at Cliveden

the joys of discovering many lovely spots. The improvements the Trust has carried out at Morden Hall Park under successive managers are good indicators of how regeneration can work and, importantly, involve a largely disaffected community. William Morris is closely connected with the Wandle, and the Trust's founders Sir Robert Hunter, Octavia Hill and Canon Rawnsley were associated with him. I like to think that the improvements would meet with their approval.

Between Petts Wood, Chislehurst and Bromley there is a remarkable urban 'lung' provided by the countryside properties of Bromley Council and the Trust. Walkers, runners, joggers, cyclists and horse-riders take full advantage of the green spaces.

Study the contrast between the manicured beauty of Cookham village and the river Thames properties and, close by, the spare countryside that is Cocks Marsh.

From Runnymede to Windsor (and back, for the energetic) the way is steeped in history. Look across from the moving memorials to President Kennedy or Commonwealth airmen on the hill to the flat meadowland of Ankerwyke. Some believe it was here that Magna Carta was signed, and there is a venerable yew that may have been growing before the birth of Christ.

Ashridge and Polesden Lacey both possess commons and a series of short walks. Ashridge is vast, and anyone completing the longest walk will have gained an overview of the Chilterns; for most of us, two or three of the short walks will probably suffice. Not so much distance to cover at Polesden, but variety and a fascinating house to explore. Both properties also offer good walks for disabled visitors.

The two walks close to each other across the Thames are memorable for the houses they pass or revolve around. Osterley is the centre of one walk and Ham the destination of the other; this walk passes, on the other bank, two magnificent properties, Syon and Marble Hill House (neither NT). The walk extends to Teddington Lock, where the river ceases to be tidal; from Osterley the route takes in the locks on the Grand Union canal.

The walk on a stretch of the River Wey Navigation begins at Dapdune Wharf, the subject of many improvements in recent years, with significant educational developments a feature, and passes through the centre of bustling Guildford to enter some tranquil countryside. Do make the detour to Shalford Mill on the return journey.

The route around Finchampstead combines notable mixed woodland and heather slopes with a charming river walk. I grew up in the area, so the rivers Blackwater and Loddon were where we paddled; unsurprisingly, I enjoyed re-discovering the placid Blackwater.

Above: Autumn on the Ashridge Estate

Water surrounds Northey Island to the extent that it is cut off at high tide. A short walk from Maldon (a town that, I am ashamed to say, was new to me), Northey is 'my sort of place', remote, full of the sounds of wildfowl, a desolate spot under wide skies, recalling those atmospheric BBC adaptations of Dickens. In the post-war years the Thames barges almost disappeared from the river and to see one was always a delight, a sort of magic mixed with nostalgia – do chat to the folk on the barges at Maldon, or to the quay master, enthusiasts all.

11

Danbury is a living history of types of commons habitat, where the Trust is managing the three commons to maintain and enhance their historic differences. Bradenham, Naphill and Downley provide more insights into the ancient rights of commoners and the effect on the land; Hughenden Manor, West Wycombe Park and the villages of West Wycombe and Bradenham (all NT) simply add to the pleasure.

Houses are pivotal to the Ightham and Chartwell walks. For pure romantic beauty, the moated houses of Baddesley Clinton, Lower Brockhampton, Little Moreton Hall and Ightham are surely unsurpassed. I never approach any of them without a shiver of anticipation and Ightham is on my shortlist of favourite properties – not to be missed. Knole never attracts deep affection (even from some of those who lived in it) but it encapsulates the history of England; Chartwell is a monument to an iconic figure of the last century.

Not much water on those walks, but at Dedham the river Stour is a constant companion. At the various centres there are always people but I much enjoyed the quiet sections from Manningtree Station to Flatford Mill, and between Dedham and Stratford St Mary where few seem to venture. Do make time to share a snack at the Flatford tea-room with the incredibly insouciant sparrows and chaffinches!

The basically sandy soils around Frensham, Witley and Milford are full of heather and gorse and are home to plant and birdlife that is generally under threat in the South East. If you are a naturalist, try to visit Thursley (not NT) – a treasure trove of species whose inclusion was prevented through shortage of space.

Dunstable Downs stand on chalk, a surface unlike any other for walking. Tricky in rain, the grass has a cushioned feel that makes it a pleasure in dry conditions – and the views are pretty impressive! The Tree Cathedral should be visited; a fine concept, it doesn't quite work for me – what do you think?

For equally spectacular views, climb Leith Hill, ideally to the top of the tower; on a fine day both the Channel and London are almost within reach.

Back in London, both the Thames Path and Hampstead walks cover places that are likely to be better known than many in the book – bringing in the Trust's properties gives, I hope, a focus to these fascinating walks, full of opportunities to admire and enjoy houses, gardens, historical sites – as well as several very modern attractions.

Last, another personal favourite, Hatfield Forest is a truly astonishing property, survivor of attempts to destroy it through the ages, and once more under threat. Stand beside one of the ancient pollarded hornbeams, look at the view and know instinctively that this is a vital piece of our natural history, history we must preserve.

Above: The South front of Hughenden Manor House

In addition to his role in founding the National Trust, Sir Robert Hunter was Secretary of the Commons Preservation Society. As such, he was responsible for saving Epping Forest from development and being responsible for defeating a Government Bill aimed at enshrining manorial rights of enclosure in law. He also played an important role in the purchase of Hindhead Common. Without Hunter's patient, precise work many of the walks I hope you will sample would not exist – the possibility that Hatfield may disappear under a runway reminds us that the need for vigilance is permanent.

Finally, from the beginnings of the National Trust there were disagreements about the balance to be struck between countryside and buildings; Octavia Hill expressed unease that her friends preferred 'beautiful open space' to 'artists'. Please look at the references to National Trust buildings along the routes. By drawing your attention to them, I hope to persuade you to combine the walks with property visits, perhaps taking a day to do so.

However you approach the walks, enjoy them!

Above: A common spotted orchid

MAKING THE MOST OF YOUR VISIT

The walks in this book have been designed for a wide range of walking abilities and to be easy to follow. At the beginning of each walk you will find the essential data – the map number and grid reference, the distance and the nature of the terrain, together with an illustrative map. Where possible we give an escape route in case you need to return more quickly than planned.

Getting there
Each walk includes details of road access and public transport services. There are now national telephone enquiry numbers for both rail and bus:
Rail: tel. 0845 748 4950. Journey planning website www.rail.co.uk/index.html
Bus: tel. 0870 608 2608

Cycling
Cycle racks are provided at NT countryside properties. For information on local cycle routes, contact Tourist Information Centres.

Safety
Ensure that someone knows where you are planning to go when you visit the countryside. Wear suitable clothing and footwear and be prepared for weather conditions to change quickly.

Follow the Countryside Code
Enjoy the countryside but please respect its life and work:
- use gates and stiles to cross fences and hedges and fasten gates after you have passed through
- protect wildlife, plants and trees and leave livestock, crops and machinery alone
- take your litter home and do not light fires

Dogs
Dogs on leads are welcome at all National Trust countryside properties. Please clean up after your dogs and use bins where provided.

For further information on National Trust properties
National Trust information line
tel. 0870 458 4000
email: enquiries@thenationaltrust.org.uk
website:www.nationaltrust.org.uk

Accommodation
National Trust Holiday Cottages brochure line tel. 0870 458 4411
email: cottages@ntrust.org.uk
www.nationaltrust.org.uk/cottages/nt.asp
B&B (NT tenants)
www.nationaltrust.org.uk/main/holidays/bed_breakfast

There is a list of useful contact details at the end of this book, on page 143.

WALK 1

CHARTWELL TO EMMETTS

Map: OS 1:25,000 Explorer 147 Sevenoaks
& Tonbridge

OS grid reference: TQ 455515

Distance: 7 miles

Terrain: Not a walk for people with mobility
impairment, as there are several stiles, steps
and steep slopes to negotiate. It can be
muddy and uneven, particularly where the
route follows bridlepaths; stout weatherproof
walking boots are strongly recommended.
Steepish climbs at the beginning of the walk,
more gradual ascents approaching Emmetts.
Dogs must be kept on leads on public roads,
and in fields with livestock.

Getting there: *Chartwell:* By train –
Edenbridge 4 miles, Edenbridge Town
4¹/₂ miles, Sevenoaks 6¹/₂ miles. By bus – from
Bromley North/South Stations to Edenbridge.
By car – 2 miles S of Westerham (A25), fork
left off B2026 after 1¹/₂ miles

Emmetts: By train – Sevenoaks, 4¹/₂ miles. By
bus – Sevenoaks to Ide Hill, 1¹/₂ miles. By car
– 1¹/₂ miles S of A25 on Sundridge/Ide Hill
road, 1¹/₂ miles N of Ide Hill off B2042

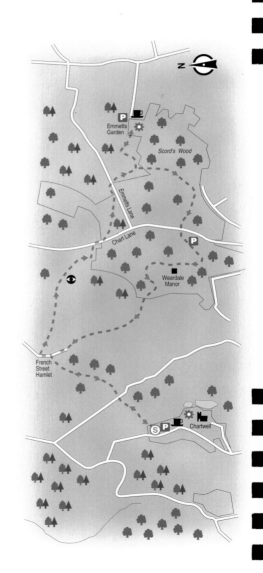

The walk, which closely follows the
waymarked Weardale Walk (leaflet
available at both properties), with
some minor variations, is a circular

route, from Chartwell to Emmetts Garden and back. It can be treated as two separate linear walks with the possibility for motorists to take two cars and leave one at each end; they may be parked at each property free of charge.

NB: The leaflet indicates one way – clockwise – to make the walk; the waymarked signs are excellent but point only in this direction. Attempting the walk anti-clockwise requires a little extra care.

A circular walk starting and finishing at Chartwell car park

▶ Leave the car park via a gate at the northwest corner, through the overflow car park and picnic field, over a stile. This is the recommended return route of the Weardale Walk, but is much better surfaced than the alternative path and has splendid views. Follow uphill before turning left and left again, over a stile by a five-barred gate onto Hosey Common Road. Bear left for about 200 yards, then right across the road and walk down the bridleway, keeping to the right at forks in the path.

At the pretty French Street Hamlet turn left onto the road. After about 65 yards, and opposite a red post-box, climb the stile on the right, and continue along the right-hand footpath. There is a steep descent of about 40 uneven steps. Negotiate another stile, walk diagonally across a field, which may have livery horses in it, and cross the bridge over a small stream.

From here the walk is largely uphill. Walk straight ahead, climbing a stile in the top right-hand corner of the field. Cross the track – the attractive vernacular buildings on the right include an NT base camp – and take the path opposite, upwards past a bench, and on to another stile. Over this, turn right and head towards a further stile at the corner of the field.

Above: Looking along the garden path towards Chartwell

Glance back for a lovely, peaceful, view over the valley.

▶ Beyond, the path continues upwards through woodland, eventually meeting a narrower path on the right; follow this path for a short way where another path crosses. Note that the route is excellently waymarked but, as it follows the Greensand Way for much of this section, there is extra guidance if needed.

Turn left and, at the next path junction, left again and cross Chart Lane (this is a busy road), taking the path opposite which leads you to Emmetts Lane.

The path passes through more old, partially coppiced woods.

This area can be very wet and an alternative is to continue right on the tarmac of Chart Lane then left along Emmetts Lane.

▶ Turn left for about 85 yards along the lane (care again); then turn right onto a footpath, past a cross path, and climb a stile to visit Emmetts.

Emmetts is a charming garden, appealing in all seasons. Paradoxically, the renowned views over the Weald are possibly better now than before the garden suffered the trauma of the great storm of 1987.

Refreshments and WC facilities are available here but please note the National Trust does ask visitors to 'report' to the ticket hut to pay/show membership cards (consult the NT Handbook for opening arrangements).

Right: The lake and house at Chartwell

▶ To continue the walk, turn left at the cross path onto the bridleway, continuing downhill through Scord's Wood. At the next two junctions continue straight ahead, following the waymarks. Turn right at the next junction and keep on this path over another intersection uphill to Chart Lane (there is a public house a little way along on the right).

Cross the road and take the path opposite, on the left of the house; turn left onto the wide path and continue past the remains of Weardale Manor on the left, which is indicated by information panels. Continue along this hard-surfaced track, keeping left until you reach a stile; cross this and continue down the road, past High View Cottage on the right.

At the next junction, turn right along the road to French Street Hamlet, and then left onto the first bridleway, from where the outward

Below: A view south to Bough Beech Reservoir at Toys Hill

journey is retraced on a steady climb uphill to Hosey Common Road. Turn left and, after 200 yards, right over a stile by the same five-barred gate to re-enter the rear of the estate. Turn right again and follow the path, admiring the views over the estate, and so back to Chartwell car park, and a visit to the house and garden.

▶ For those not yet satisfied, there is a further walk, the Chartwell Estate Walk, which has more steep slopes, and steps, but offers equally superb views of Chartwell and the Weald. The woodlands of the estate are particularly lovely in spring, with both bluebells and foxgloves. Ask at the visitor's entrance kiosk for a map.

 Chartwell was the home of Sir Winston Churchill from 1924 until his death. The terraced garden, with lawns, orchard, roses and water garden, enjoys fine views over the Weald of Kent.

 Refreshments, including full meals, are available in the restaurant. Also WCs.

Above: A sea of bluebells in Emmetts Garden

WALK 2

RUNNYMEDE, SAVILL GARDENS & WINDSOR GREAT PARK

Map: OS 1:25,000 Explorer 160 Windsor, Weybridge & Bracknell

OS grid reference: TQ 007720

Distance: Runnymede walk 6 miles; Windsor walk 13 miles

Terrain: Varied. Flat, easy in the meadows, can be very wet. Steepish climb up steps to Kennedy Memorial area, steep up to Cooper's Hill, more gentle slope down to the Great Park, which is flat with a good surface. Some paved roads.

Getting there: By train – Egham ¹/₂ mile

By bus – Staines/Colnbrook

By car – M25 J13, A308 2 miles W of Runnymede Bridge

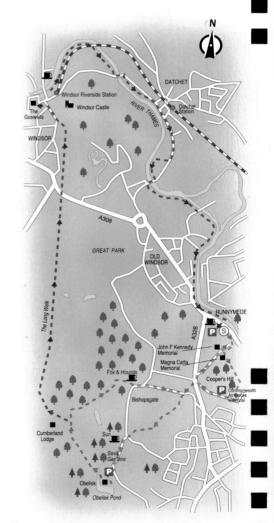

There is an enormous choice for the walker in this area and we include recommendations for several National Trust walks. For a longer walk, we have incorporated historic Runnymede meadows and the Magna Carta (see page 128), Kennedy and Air Forces Memorials before passing the Savill Gardens into part of the Great Park. Here there is an opportunity for a much longer walk to Windsor or return to Runnymede. All the walks are described as starting from the

Key

▬ ▬ ▬ Runnymede Circular Walks

▬ ▬ ▬ Runnymede via Commonwealth Air Forces Memorial to Windsor Great Park

National Trust car park (charge) at the Magna Carta tea-room in the Fairhaven Lodge at the Windsor end of the Runnymede stretch of the Old Windsor Road (A308), bordering the river Thames.

The Magna Carta tea-room is often busy but serves good food.

Circular walks at Runnymede

The National Trust suggests several walks here: one takes in a climb through the woods to the Kennedy Memorial, and the American Bar Association Memorial to Magna Carta, returning across the meadow and along the river bank (can be wet, at times impassable) back to the car park (an audio tape may be available – please enquire).

The Trust's Yellow Walk takes 2¹/₂ hours and skirts the Magna Carta Memorial and Cooper's Hill Woods, continuing around the ponds in Langham Meadow. This marshy area is a Site of Special Scientific Interest, and the haunt of herons, kingfishers and many species of dragonfly. The walk continues through the hay meadow, with its diversity of plant and insect life, and returns along the bank of the Thames past a creek known as the Lily Pond, frequented by a variety of wildfowl.

From Runnymede via the Commonwealth Air Forces Memorial to Windsor Great Park

The Trust's Purple Walk takes two hours and passes the Magna Carta Memorial, through Cooper's Hill Woods and up to the poignant Air Forces Memorial for those who have no known grave, with its commanding view at the top of the hill. The choices here are to return down the hill and through the woods to the meadows and back to the car park, or to extend the walk as we suggest below.

▶ From the Air Forces Memorial turn right and pass the car park on the left (free parking here – a possible starting point for the walk) and the buildings of Brunel University on the right. Continue along Cooper's Hill

Above: Langham Pond

Lane, bearing left and crossing over the busy A238 into Castle Hill Road (signed to Savill Gardens). Proceed straight over Bishopsgate Road into Ham Lane, a private road but usable by pedestrians. Go downhill between houses on a reasonable path and take the signposted footpath at the bottom of the lane. This passes between fields and woods (care needed at the latter stages where the path is steep and eroded by water) before joining a tarmac road – Prospect Lane – between some attractive cottages, and reaching the main road at the Sun pub.

The next section, left past the pub, can be a little tricky. There is no pavement for almost ½ mile and the road is narrow, with speeding cars.

Take the first entrance, to the coach park, at the Savill Gardens and, if time permits, explore this

lovely garden, famous for its rhododendrons – or walk through the car park (another possible starting point – charge) to the entrance leading into the Great Park and towards the Obelisk and the Obelisk Pond. There are paths all round this lake, which supports a variety of wildfowl and fish including carp and tench.

The pollarding of trees as a protection against livestock means they can live to a great age and will become attractive to a great many species. (For more on this see article p.40).

For birdwatchers the Great Park, with its patches of ancient woodland including oak planted from Elizabethan times onwards, is a pleasure at all seasons. Look for parties of siskin in winter, nuthatch, all three woodpecker species and, in summer, the handsome hobby. Summer also sees more than 30 butterfly species including white admiral, several blues and five types of skipper. Rare fungi are often associated with old trees, while the list of beetles identified in the Park is truly remarkable – over 2,000 species.

▶ The walk turns towards the corner of Savill Gardens over an ornamental bridge, from which it is possible to peer into the garden, and passes the edge of Smith's Lawn, home to some of the most prestigious polo competitions played in Britain. Continue past Cumberland Lodge before turning right towards Bishopsgate.

The Fox & Hounds in Bishopsgate serves good-quality food.

Above: The Magna Carta Memorial, designating the spot where the document was sealed in 1225.

▶ Walk along Bishopsgate Road – tarmac, but with a pavement and a wide grass verge – back to Castle Hill Road, returning either to Cooper's Lane car park or, at the A238, turn left and shortly right, taking the signed path back to Runnymede via the Kennedy Memorial (steps down).

For the determined walker there is a longer walk (13 miles) beginning at Runnymede. The first part of the walk is as described above but, at Cumberland Lodge continue ahead, leaving the Lodge and Royal School on the left, to join the Three Castles Path (better known to many as the Long Walk!) close to the Ox Pond. Turn north and walk towards the Castle, about 3 miles. On arrival, head left of the castle to a three-acre property that many of the National Trust's own staff would have difficulty identifying. This is The Goswells, between Thames Street and the Thames, and it would seem churlish not to interrupt the walk with a brief stroll round it! It is, of

Below: Runnymede is an area of riverside meadows, grassland and woodland, part SSSI, rich in flora and fauna.

course, perfectly feasible to start and end this walk from one of the stations in Windsor.

To return to Runnymede join the Thames Path just north-east of The Goswells and follow it along the loop in the Thames, crossing the river at Datchet. Continue along the waymarked path, re-crossing at Albert Bridge and eventually, past Old Windsor, entering Runnymede – about 5½ miles.

Below: The John F. Kennedy memorial, erected in 1965 to honour the American President.

WALK 3

IGHTHAM MOTE TO KNOLE

Map: OS 1:25,000 Explorer 147 Sevenoaks & Tonbridge

OS grid reference: TQ 585535

Distance: 3³/₄ miles; 7 miles

Terrain: Undulating, some steep sections. Poor-quality paths, difficult stiles and muddy areas (most in the first section to One Tree Hill). Knole Park is a good area for walking. Stout footwear required at all seasons with a walking stick a useful accessory.

Getting there: *Ightham*: By train – Borough Green & Wrotham 3¹/₂ miles, Hildenborough 4 miles. By bus – services to & from Tunbridge Wells, Sevenoaks, Shipbourne, Gravesend. By car – off A25, 2¹/₂ miles S of Ightham, off A227. Free parking at Ightham Mote, daily dawn to dusk.

Knole: By train – Sevenoaks 1¹/₂ miles. By bus – Bromley North & South Stations – Tunbridge Wells. By car – M25 J5, A23 S, follow signs for Sevenoaks & Knole (off A225 in town).

This an ideal walk for those who can leave a car at either end of the route.

Ightham Mote is one of the Trust's most enduringly romantic properties. From it the walk, along the long-distance Greensand Way Path, passes through One Tree Hill, with

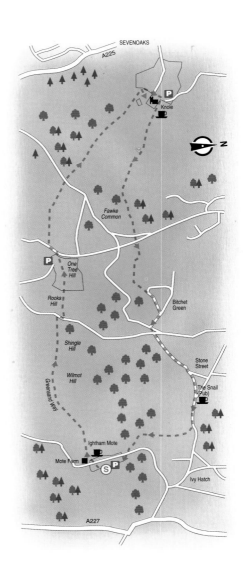

its fine viewpoint, then into the deer park, to end at Knole, a fascinating survivor of great house splendour and a huge contrast to the intimacy of Ightham.

A linear walk starting at Ightham Mote and ending at Knole

▶ The walk we recommend begins at Ightham Mote, taking the footpath from the edge of the car park. Drop downhill, past the 14th-century moated manor house, turning right onto a road (there are signs here to other paths – see below) and walk past the end of the house, turning

left at the metalled gates leading into the garden.

At the main road the walk joins the Greensand Way. Turn briefly right then left past Mote Farm, following the path for a little way before glancing back to enjoy an archetypal Kentish view of farm buildings and an oast-house, before walking along a wide track between hedgerows. Variable in quality, it drops steadily downhill to the truly delightful Wilmot Cottage with, beyond it, a brick building housing a spring. Soon there are fine views on the left before the 'Green Route No 3' turns off to the right, leading eventually back to the car park.

Continue along the foot of Shingle Hill, taking care with the rocks, which are scattered along the route, and past some rather scrubby fields, until reaching a stile in poor repair. Turn right, walking a few yards uphill on a tarmac road before, opposite a gate and private garage, turning left and clambering up five steep, uneven steps.

As the path begins to climb through Rooks Hill Wood there are steep drops on the left to undulating farmland and tantalising views of the Weald, often interrupted by fairly dense stands of trees (take care on this difficult path, where exposed

Above: Looking through the Outer Hall window to the Courtyard at Ightham Mote.

Right: Ightham Mote, one of the Trust's most romantic properties.

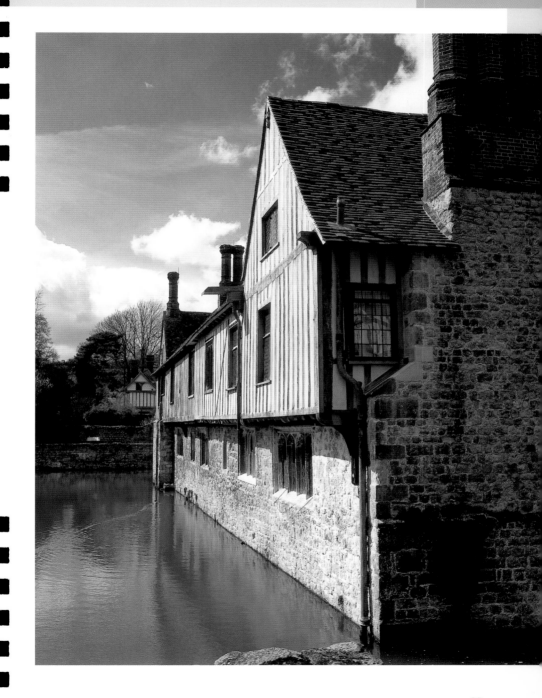

tree roots and water have deeply scarred the track). Eventually, the long, awkward climb is rewarded by arriving at the superb viewpoint of One Tree Hill.

This broad-leaved, partly coppiced woodland is probably at its best in spring and early summer, but the views over the Kentish Weald are just as spectacular in winter.

▶ Follow the waymarked path, dropping down to reach, and pass over, the unclassified road (this is tricky – a combination of traffic, blind corner and a few yards of steep downhill slope). Turn left on the road then angle right as if

Above: Autumn on the Knole estate

Right: The West Front at Knole

entering the gates of Shepherd's Mead before taking the Greensand Way along the edge of the garden of the estate. Walk uphill, passing through a yew tunnel and continue between a wood and a field before dropping through part of Redlands Wood to cross another unclassified road. Pass through a large stile-cum-kissing gate into the magnificent deer park that surrounds Knole (NB: do not feed the deer, as they can be dangerous). Many of the saplings seen throughout the park were planted to replace trees lost in the 1987 storm.

The original 15th-century house was enlarged in the late 16th century and has remained largely unaltered since. Portraits, furniture, silver, tapestries and textiles crowd the rooms open to the public. It is the home of the Sackville family (see p.128).

▶ The Greensand Way passes the front of the house, swinging left down and then uphill to Sevenoaks High Street (A225) where it is possible, if Knole is shut, to find refreshments.

Refreshments and visitor facilities are available at both Ightham Mote and Knole.

For the enthusiastic walker – or one who has no form of transport back to Ightham! – the following is a possible extension.

▶ From the back of Knole house proceed east, taking a right fork in the path and passing three small ponds. Take a left fork, across Fawke Common. Cross two unclassified roads and follow paths towards Bitchet Green. Part of this route is on made-up roads. Turn sharp right at Bitchet Green hamlet, joining the unclassified road to Stone Street and Ivy Hatch (care needed here).

At the junction with Stone Street is the interestingly named Snail public house – fish is a speciality here.

▶ Turn right towards Ivy Hatch and, in another 100 yards or so, take the bridleway on the right. This leads to Ightham, entering the property close to Scathes Wood. A short walk down the drive and the car park is reached. **NB:** There is a wheelchair-accessible walk of 1½ miles through Scathes Wood, Ightham. Disabled people may park in the gateway; call the House for the gate combination. The Trust requests that the gate be locked behind users of this route. The 1½-mile extension of this walk is not suitable for wheelchair users.

WALK 4

HATFIELD FOREST

Maps: OS 1:25,000 Explorer 183 Chelmsford & The Rodings; 195 Braintree & Saffron Walden

OS grid reference: TL 540198

Distance: 1/2 miles; 4/2 miles

Terrain: Flat, mostly easy, can be very wet, muddy. Parts may be under cultivation at some times of the year

Getting there: By train – Bishop's Stortford 4 miles; also at Chelmsford, Elsenham, Stansted Airport

By bus – Chelmsford–Stansted Airport; Bishop's Stortford–Great Dunmow; Bishop's Stortford–Elsenham: alight Green Man Takeley, thence 1/2 mile

By car – off A120 signed at Takeley, E of Bishop's Stortford

During the season, please park in the nearby car park and not on the wayside. In winter, cars must be parked at the entrance car park. A boardwalk route is planned to ease access to the Shell House.

There is a refreshment kiosk nearby and other visitor facilities including WCs and wheelchair- and pushchair-accessible picnic tables. A leaflet, describing the particular points of interest visible from the numbered posts along the walk, is available from the kiosk.

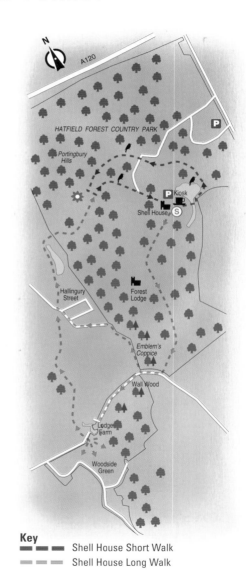

Key

━ ━ ━ Shell House Short Walk

╍ ╍ ╍ Shell House Long Walk

33

This outstanding area of ancient woodland, rich in wildlife, is a magnificent survival of a system of land-use in existence long before the Norman kings claimed it as a Royal Forest. The earthwork on Portingbury Hill may be Iron Age in origin. There is excellent, unhindered walking along the many chases and rides. We suggest two walks, the leafleted Nature Trail, and a second, longer walk which explores a wider area, including the unusually large village common at Woodside Green. As Hatfield is a focal point of several recreational paths (the Forest Way, Harcamlow Way and Three Forests Way), we have incorporated parts of these waymarked routes in the second walk.

A circular walk starting and ending at the Shell House

NB: Part of this waymarked trail is accessible to wheelchair users in dry weather.

The 'small house' is a rare example of a mid-18th-century 'picnic room' – used by the Houblon family (the then owners of much of the Forest) to entertain friends to tea by the newly created lake in the middle of the forest. The use of shells and shell motifs was fashionable at this time, and it is believed one of the daughters was responsible for the decoration. The name was changed, but the function of the Shell House remains broadly the same.

▶ From the kiosk walk past the Shell House, towards the dam at the end of

the lake. Because of the number of visitors, this area can be muddy and, although the ducks and Canada geese are popular with visitors, they do leave deposits – care needs to be taken. Walking along the dam, notice the three Ice Age boulders in the water.

Air bubbles rising to the surface near to the weeds are an indication that tench – prevalent here – may be feeding. Common tern, hovering and diving for fish, are worth looking for in spring, while the courting ritual of the great crested grebe is an early summer highlight. The resident mallard, moorhen and coot may be joined, in winter, by tufted duck and pochard.

▶ At the end of the dam, the walk passes, for the first time, among specimens of the two great trees of the forest, oak and hornbeam. As the walk turns away from the lake, the surface improves, becoming short, springy turf for some time.

The National Trust has re-introduced the ancient practice of coppicing and pollarding trees (see feature on p.40) in parts of the Forest but these have not been coppiced – regularly cut to the ground to provide materials for fencing, fuel and thatching – for many years.

▶ At Post 4 the twin trunks of the oak are confirmation that it was once coppiced. Some aircraft noise is apparent along the walk, particularly hereabouts. Near Post 5 is a group of conifers, pine and cedars with, at the edge of the Elgin Coppice (6), the sparse remains of a stone pine. Presumably this, with the Austrian and Corsican pine in the earlier group, was part of a deliberate, if bizarre, attempt to create a Mediterranean atmosphere

Below: Hatfield Forest, an outstanding area of ancient woodland, rich in wildlife.

in an archetypal English landscape. At Post 7 are the remains of old gravel workings, now just a series of humps and hollows, home to plants not found elsewhere in the Forest, including harebells.

Just below this is the Marsh, a managed area of marshland, supporting a variety of plants, birds and insects.

The tall, bulrush-like plant is reedmace, on which it may be possible to see the handsome, black-headed reed bunting perching and singing. Reed and sedge warblers are less visible; like them, the water rail – with its range of grunts and squeals, most frequently likened to a piglet – may be heard, but is one of our most elusive birds.

Below: The Trust has reintroduced the ancient practice of coppicing in parts of the Forest.

Left: Looking up through the branches of an ornamental plane tree

▶ Beyond Post 8, close to a 300-year-old pollarded hornbeam, the path crosses the road known as London Road and claimed to be part of the ancient coach route from East Anglia to London. The nearby bridge is called London Bridge. Continuing through an area of heathland with a relatively new plantation of sweet chestnut on the left, the route passes a redundant badger sett, and several mounds, the nests of yellow meadow ants. The trail crosses Shermore Brook, sometimes little more than mud, but with watercress and the large yellow flowers of creeping jenny in summer, and then follows woodland rides edged with thick clumps of blackthorn, rich with sloes in summer. The rides are edged by old hazel coppice with clear ground beneath the trees.

Above: Southern marsh orchid

In a clearing further along (Post 12), the Iron Age settlement of Portingbury Hills has a large variety of wild flowers.

✿ Some orchids grow here, but cowslip, valerian and many others are more common. Butterflies, particularly meadow brown and common blue, flourish in this open area.

🐦 Fallow, the original deer of the Forest, and muntjac, a relative newcomer, sometimes appear in this area, while the glorious song of the nightingale can be heard throughout the day in early summer.

The area between (12) and (13) is heavily wooded and coppiced; it can be very muddy and progress may be easier under the trees.

▶ At (13) (see also longer walk, opposite) the walk turns back along a wide grassy ride (more, very active, meadow brown butterflies) with trees including silver birch and ash. There is a drainage ditch here, attractive to several plant species, including primrose and violets in spring and the pink flowers of centaury in summer.

Turn right between the old gate posts towards the very visible divided ash (14) – this section can be muddy. An even more commanding landmark is the stately horse chestnut tree (15) across a large, grassy, open area. Here the walk rejoins the road back to the Shell House, diverting left through a gate to finish by the magnificent oak (16) close to the kiosk where the food is simple but, when we visited, was excellent!

A longer circular walk, including Woodside Green, starting and ending at the Shell House

▶ From the Shell House and car park, walk south west towards Forest Lodge, a 16th-century house (not open to the public), built for the foresters, which probably had a viewing tower to allow a view of the central plain.

Join the waymarked Forest Way trail, heading south along this clearly defined route for almost a mile. Beyond a stile there is an excellent lay-by, with parking for two cars should the main car park be closed (in winter). The route turns right along the road, reaching a second lay-by on a difficult blind corner of the road a hundred yards or so ahead. At this point the route turns north up a footpath, known as West Ride, with Emblem's Coppice on the right.

For those interested in visiting Woodside Green (NT), continue on the Forest Way as it follows the road, passing the attractive grouping of houses at Lodge Farm. Wall Wood (NT) is on the left of the road, ending by the cattle grid. Continue on the road, noting the footpath signpost on the right, a possible extension of the walk. On the left now is the large open space of Woodside Green, which is well worth the detour (note that neither Woodfold nor Monk's

Wood belongs to the Trust and visitors are deterred).

▶ Go back to the signpost and choose between the alternatives – north along the footpath, or back along the road to the West Ride footpath.

Although not marked as such, the signpost indicates the route of both the Harcamlow and Three Forests Way north across (cropped) fields and past Whitegate Plantation to Hallingbury Street. At Hallingbury Street, where the route is not clearly marked, go forward at signs to Marston Farm, the Forge and Rotarua – this is the point where the alternative routes re-unite.

▶ For those walking directly up West Ride, the path turns left towards Hallingbury Street at Leaper's Lane (can be very muddy). The route joins a tarmac road, the Street, and then turns right at the signs for Marston Farm. Here it joins the route from Woodside Common and proceeds past a lake before, at Beggar's Hall, following the waymarks back into the Forest.

The route is beside the drainage ditch and, at Round Coppice, it joins Walk 1 at Post 13 (see above) and follows the same route past Posts 14–16 back to the Shell House and the car park.

WOODLAND & FOREST

When you walk round some of the properties covered in these walks you get a fascinating glimpse into the history of our woodlands. Ancient woodlands, those that have been continuously wooded for a minimum of three or four centuries, and secondary woodlands from more recent times are present, sometimes on the same walk.

The old woods are beautiful places in which to walk, containing rare or unusual species of birds, plants, fungi and insects. Some plants, known as indicators, have been used to identify the age of woods; if herb Paris, woodruff, yellow pimpernel and small teasel

Above: Runnymede: a dead tree on the edge of Cooper's Hill Wood.

are found in a wood, it is probably ancient woodland. Trees like wild service and small-leaved lime (once the most widespread tree in British woods) provide further evidence. For secondary woods, the indicators include ivy, herb bennet and lords and ladies.

Coppicing and pollarding, which have been practised for centuries, probably since Neolithic times, help to preserve many woods that might otherwise have disappeared. Most broadleaved trees do not die when cut down and trees such as oak, ash, hazel and hornbeam send up new shoots, known as coppice. The shoots were 'farmed' to produce timber for fences and firewood. One great benefit of coppicing is that trees react by producing more vigorous growth and live longer than if left to mature naturally – in fact all the oldest trees in Britain have grown from coppice 'stools', as the cut stumps are known.

Woods were cut in rotation, supplying annual timber requirements for commoners (see p.108). Coppicing continued until the end of the 19th century, when coal replaced charcoal as a cheap fuel. Today, the practice is undergoing something of a revival and the National Trust now coppices several of the woods mentioned in these walks.

Pollarding is more difficult than coppicing, as trees are cut about 15 feet above ground level to prevent deer and domestic animals from browsing the regenerating shoots. The characteristic pollarded tree develops a large knobbly growth; it is not restricted to woodland – the river Stour is lined with pollards.

Forests were large, unenclosed areas over which the king asserted his right to hunt. Forest laws, introduced by the Normans, considerably extended the size of the forests and included many restrictions on those who owned or claimed commoners' rights over the land. Today, forests may appear rather untidy, with scrubby open spaces and varied woodland, but they often contain marvellous pockets of ancient, often oak, woodland.

Hatfield Forest was the last royal forest to be enclosed and, unlike most newly enclosed forests, suffered precious little change. In the coppices, the ancient woodland trees survive, some giant oak and hornbeam stools among them. The coppices are separated by open spaces or 'plains' grazed by a combination of fallow deer and, in summer, cattle – much as many of the forests and woods were in the Middle Ages. The woodlands remain rich in plants, birdlife and insects, including many rarities, while recent work by the National Trust has improved the condition of the plains and their plants.

Below: Hatfield Forest

WALK 5

BRADENHAM & WEST WYCOMBE

Map: OS 1:25,000 Explorer 172 Chiltern Hills East

OS grid reference: SU 866955

Distance: approx 8 miles, but see text

Terrain: Undulating, quite hilly in places, not easy, some level walking on Chiltern Ridge, which can be wet, even in summer. Some paved roads. Heavily wooded in parts, can be cool even on warm days – sensible clothing required at all seasons.

Getting there: *Hughenden*: By train – High Wycombe 2 miles. By bus – Aylesbury/High Wycombe (long, steep walk to house)
By car – 1½ miles N of High Wycombe, W of A4128

West Wycombe: By train – High Wycombe 2½ miles. By bus – Oxford/High Wycombe and Thame/High Wycombe (all buses pass near High Wycombe Station)
By car – 2 miles W of High Wycombe on A40

Bradenham: By train – Saunderton 1 mile
By bus – Princes Risborough/High Wycombe
By car – 4 miles NW of High Wycombe, off A4010

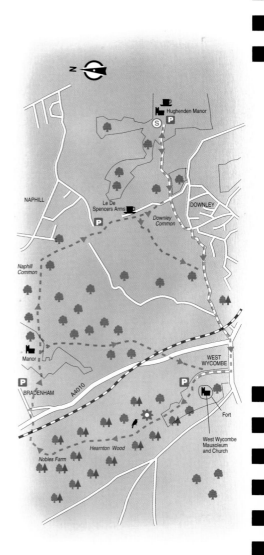

This walk has the great advantage of being accessible at a large number of points, making it equally convenient for those arriving on foot or using public or private transport. Park at Hughenden Manor, in West Wycombe, or Bradenham and pick up the path.

A delightful walk, adapted from the excellent NT leaflet and encompassing a great variety of NT properties; common land (see p.108), estate villages, beech woods, viewpoints, the house and garden of Benjamin and Mary Anne Disraeli and the remarkable Italianate conceit of West Wycombe Park.

A circular walk starting and ending in Hughenden car park

▶ From Hughenden, follow the bridleway signs downhill to Downley village (there are large, loose flints and tree roots at the foot of the valley). This is the point to which the circular walk returns. At a tarmac road – Moor Lane – proceed ahead and, near the post office, go ahead again on a footpath. Take the right-hand path beyond the school entrance. Drop downhill for about half a mile through a narrow, tunnel-like section, widening to an area where there is a fine view of West Wycombe Mausoleum and Church high on the ridge ahead.

Red kite can often be seen riding the thermals in this valley.

Right: The entrance to Hughenden Manor. The gates are topped by the letters 'D' for Disraeli and 'B' for his title Earl of Beaconsfield.

▶ At the narrow tarmac road bear left, under a railway bridge, to the difficult roundabout junction of the A40/A4010. Take great care crossing the road, then walk on into West Wycombe village.

Both the village and West Wycombe Park, seat of the Dashwood family, belong to the National Trust. Sir Francis Dashwood, founder of the Dilettanti Society and the Hellfire Club, created the rococo landscaped garden in the mid-18th century.

There are several pubs and other eating places in this lovely village.

▶ Beside the post office, turn right under the village clock, under the arch and up Church Lane. Walk up the hill, taking the first opening in the hedge on the left to the top of the hill.

This hill is the site of an Iron Age hill-fort.

Above: The monument, commemorating Benjamin Disraeli's father Isaac, was built in 1862 by E.B. Lamb.

▶ Skirt round the mausoleum and church (neither they, nor the infamous Hellfire Caves, belong to the Trust but are worth a detour) and follow the sign to Saunderton, pausing to enjoy the views of the valleys below, before joining a level track on top of the ridge. The path, wide and well defined, continues parallel to, but well above, the A4010 (some traffic noise and occasional train sounds).

Potentially fine views are frequently blocked by necessary tree regeneration. Happily, frustration quickly gives way to pleasure as the mature mixed species – conifer, hazel, oak – in Hearnton Wood are home, in season, to a wide range of woodland birds and butterflies. In addition, rosebay willowherb along with various umbellifers fringe the route. The path through the woods can be muddy with large puddles.

▶ Ignore signs that refer to the 'circular walk' on both left and right and, after about a mile, the walk passes Nobles Farm, a pleasant grouping of buildings. Here the path turns sharp right, down through a steep, difficult, beech coppice. Next a stile, a field and another stile with fine views of the Church and Manor of Bradenham across the valley before a grassland field with typical flowers – clover and scabious – leads to the busy railway line. Great care is needed crossing the line, and the A4010 beyond it. Pass the Red Lion and start up Bradenham Woods Lane.

Prominently displayed at the edge of the common, on the right, is an Iron Age sarsen stone, placed here by the Parish Council to commemorate the start of the new millennium.

Higher up is the cricket green, set on a marvellous slope – balls struck towards the upper green must pull up very quickly, while those hit downhill probably endanger traffic on the A4010!

▶ Keep on past the wall of the manor house and soon, at a fork in the track, there are two choices – the short walk back through woodland along a narrow, waymarked path to West Wycombe, or the continuation of the long walk. Whichever route is taken, a great part will be in wooded land, much of it beech.

The trees hereabouts are mostly about 120 years old, and were planted to provide timber for the local furniture trade, still flourishing in the High Wycombe area today. A workshop in Church Lane, West Wycombe, uses local beech in its furniture.

Below: Hughenden Manor was the home of Benjamin Disraeli from 1848 until his death in 1881.

The National Trust has owned most of the village since 1956, including the Manor House, once the home of Benjamin's father, Isaac D'Israeli (let, not open), which is passed on the left as the walk continues to a gravel track at the top of the Green.

▶ For the short walk, take the narrow path to the right of the fork, follow the waymarks for about three-quarters of a mile, drop into the valley, once again taking care when re-crossing the railway and road, and follow the path uphill through fields. At the top, Church Lane is rejoined; follow the tarmac road downhill under the clock arch to the

village. The total circuit – West Wycombe/Bradenham/West Wycombe – is about 3½ miles.

For those wishing to start and finish at Bradenham, and willing to omit Wycombe, turn back uphill at Church Lane, joining the long walk near to the mausoleum and returning via the Nobles Farm section (see above).

▶ To continue with the long walk, follow the right fork of the track quite steeply uphill towards Naphill Common (the surface is quite loose). The brick and flint cottages on the right are typical of the vernacular buildings of the area. There are a variety of paths crossing Naphill Common, a traditional wood pasture, pollarded for timber and grazed by commoners' animals (see article p.108). Pollarding here is not as obvious as at Hatfield (see p.33) and the undergrowth on the common is quite dense, with bracken and holly scrub prominent.

The route is almost due east; follow the waymarked signs with the aim of reaching the roughly north/south path a little below Naphill village. Past a pond, the route turns right, downhill through woodland (used, near Hunt's Hill, by young mountain bikers) before reaching Downley Common with its cricket green.

Originally summer pasture for West Wycombe, grazing over Downley Common died out in the 19th century; as a result, the trees here are younger than those on Bradenham and Naphill.

The interestingly named pub, the Le De Spencers Arms, serves traditional ales and food in its dark, wooden bars.

From the pub, continue downhill, passing houses on the left before entering woodland. At the foot of the valley, where there is an NT Omega sign, four paths meet. Take the bridleway signed to Hughenden and follow it, returning uphill to the estate.

Lunches, teas and snacks are available in the restaurant.

For those planning to start the walk elsewhere, take the road round the cricket green, turning right along a narrow footpath beside a cottage. Level at first, it passes between tall hedgerows before dropping downhill – with a brief glimpse of the mausoleum in a gap in the hedge – to link with the path that comes down from Downley village beside a flight of steps leading nowhere in particular! Soon the open fields are reached with the possibility of sighting red kites (see p.43) and the walk is followed into West Wycombe and to whichever starting point was used.

WALK 6

POLESDEN LACEY ESTATE

Map: OS 1:25,000 Explorer 146 Dorking, Box Hill & Reigate
OS grid reference: TQ136522 – Polesden Lacey car park
Distance: 3 miles
Terrain: Varied, most on good surfaces. Some long climbs. The wooded area of Ranmore Common can be wet.
Getting there: By train – Box Hill & Westhumble station (cycle hire at the station), Leatherhead, Effingham
By bus – Guildford–Leatherhead (alight in Great Bookham)
By car – A246 Leatherhead–Guildford, property is 2 miles S (signed in Great Bookham)

This estate on the north slopes of the North Downs in Surrey is comprised of 560 hectares (1,385 acres) of woods, farmland and formal gardens surrounding a Regency villa, substantially re-modelled in the Edwardian era by the society hostess Mrs Greville. The NT has created several landscape walks around the estate; the most recent samples Ranmore Common, the large wooded area visible looking south from Polesden Lacey.

Key

▰ ▰ ▰ Circular Estate Walk
▰ ▰ ▰ Other Walks

A leaflet guide including maps and points of interest is available from the Polesden Lacey shop.

NB: Walkers are asked to note that they are sharing parts of these paths with horse-riders, cyclists and other vehicles. Well-controlled dogs are welcome on these walks except in the walled garden.

A circular walk around the estate beginning at the Polesden Lacey car park

We suggest a circular walk, based around the NT's Prospect Lodge Walk and the continuation to Yew Tree Farm with possible extensions to Ranmore Common.

Above: A colourful herbaceous border at Polesden Lacey

▶ Starting at the car park, walk downhill, admiring the house, before turning left along the terrace and through the colonnade, originally the portico to the house, joining Bagden Drive and walking down a steep hill to a gate (here the Polesden Valley walk turns right).

Continue southwest along Connicutt Lane, gradually bearing right, with Ranmore Wood on the left.

The charming small cottage, Tanner's Hatch, one of the smallest hostels owned by the Youth Hostels Association, is at least 400 years old. The next cottage, Prospect Lodge, is Victorian but thought to be on the site of the medieval Polesden.

Across the lane is a magnificent view of Polesden Lacey.

▶ For a shorter walk, turn right at this point and walk past Polesden Farm, where the Prospect Valley Walk is rejoined, leading to the house and car park. The longer walk turns south, through woodland, towards Ranmore Common, turning right by a superb old beech tree (this is another point of access for those walking to or from the Ranmore car parks).

Right: The original Regency house was extensively remodelled in 1906–9 by the Hon. Mrs Ronald Greville, a well-known Edwardian hostess.

After the route joins Yewtree Lane, there are fine views of the House, and of Effingham Hill and Box Hill at either end of Polesden Valley.

▶ At Yewtree Farm, the route turns left through fields to join Hogden Lane, probably the route for taking pigs to feed on the common. The road curves gently uphill to the right; at the arrow, go left into the former kitchen garden, now a pasture full of flowers in spring and summer, including vetch, geranium and spurge. (Here the route rejoins the Polesden Valley Walk.)

Leave this garden, crossing an attractive thatched bridge over Yewtree Lane to enter the walled garden, started in the 17th century, re-built in the 19th and re-designed by Mrs Greville in the early 20th century. (Dog owners are requested to avoid the walled flower garden and follow the arrows through the kitchen garden to the visitor facilities and the car park.)

Through this garden, and behind the House, in the Stable Yard, is the restaurant and shop; continue for the car park.

Other walks

The Polesden Valley Walk, though shorter, covers part of the route given above, passing through the valley, below the Terrace to Polesden Farm before heading uphill along Yewtree Lane to the gardens.

The Admiral's Walk is a short walk, approximately one mile, much of it on a hardened track. The longer walk was developed to allow wheelchair users, preferably accompanied by a strong pusher, to enjoy the wonderful views from the grounds around the House. There are some lengthy inclines, mostly gentle, but requiring care.

▶ The walk starts at the end of the car park and turns immediately left. At the first fork, branch right, glancing back to enjoy the view of the house.

Above: A view through beech trees at Polesden Lacey

Go through a gate into a field (wheelchair users will notice a slight camber), pausing to look at the spire of Ranmore Church rising above the trees. The deep bridleway crossed after negotiating two more gates is Connicutt Lane and the path now passes through Freehold Wood before, close by a fallen tree – useful for sitting on – there is a fleeting view of Box Hill. Skirt the old chalk

Below: A carpet of bluebells on Ranmore Common

pit and notice the flowers in this area, including bugle and speedwell, before turning back uphill along Bagden Drive, in use until the 1940s as the main approach to the house from Box Hill & Westhumble station (it is still the route for those arriving on foot from the station).

Beyond the stone bridge, there is a choice of return route towards the house; continuing along the Drive or taking the grassy path along the Terrace with wonderful views over Ranmore. Near the colonnade the Trust has created an opening to the terrace suitable for push- and wheelchairs; we suggest this as a slight variation to the printed route. Both routes meet a wide tarmac road and turn right to the car park.

We end with the newest walk, centred on the car parks along Ranmore Common Road. The route begins at a point opposite one of these, on the northern side of the road (TQ 141504). It is possible to park here and walk up the various tracks leading to Tanner's Hatch, Prospect Lodge or Yewtree Farm, continuing with the walk through the gardens, past the house (see route above), before returning to this car park.

▶ The waymarked walk travels west, at first on a broad grassy track through the ancient woodland of the Common, crossing many paths and bridleways. The advantage for the novice walker is that, at almost any time, it is possible to turn left and regain Ranmore Common Road. Most of the paths on Ranmore have been signed, encouraging visitors to walk at will over the common while not feeling lost.

 Deer are quite often seen along the route as it leads through mixed woodland with some delightful clearings. Bluebells dominate in spring, but there are many other wild flowers – deadnettle, masses of bugle – and mature trees, including May, almost overpoweringly scented in early summer.

At one point, the walk drops down into Ash Valley (can be wet) crossing one of several paths leading up to Tanner's Hatch. Shortly, the path turns left by Lonesome Cottage (not NT) and then passes Hogden Cottage before returning to the road.

To return to the car park follow the broad bridleway beside Ranmore Common Road.

WALK 7

ASHRIDGE ESTATE

Map: OS 1:25,000 Explorer 181 Chiltern Hills North

OS grid reference: Monument SP970131; Steps Hill car park SP963156

Distance: from ¹/₂ mile to 16 miles

Terrain: Varied, mostly unmade paths. Some flat, but several steep climbs. Wooded area around Monument often wet and can be very muddy. Stout footwear recommended.

Getting there: By train – Tring (Monument), Cheddington (Beacon)

By car – Monument – B4506 (car park signed from road); Beacon – Beacon Road (off B4506 at Ringshall to Steps Hill car park SP966159)

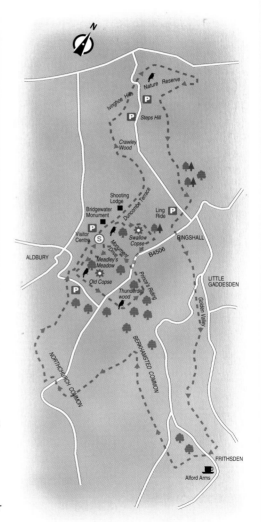

This vast tract of National Trust downland, commons and woods on the eastern ridge of the Chiltern Hills offers an abundance of different kinds of walk, from the long Boundary Trail down to the half-mile route around Meadley's Meadow. Leaflets are available from the Visitor Centre for all named walks.

A series of circular walks starting and ending at the Visitor Centre

The freedom to wander at will is one of the special attractions of this fascinating estate. Nonetheless, the following routes are recommended for their specific appeal.

Two self-guided trails have been created particularly for families – one two-mile route along Duncombe Terrace, and a circular route of about half a mile around Meadley's Meadow, beginning and ending at the Visitor Centre. This route is particularly suitable for wheel- and powered chairs, but also for anyone

Above: Muntjac and fallow deer can often be seen feeding.

who prefers a stable surface. Good in all seasons, and an ideal area to study the beech, the most important tree of the Chilterns, the path progresses through a shimmering haze of blue when the bluebells are out.

▶ Leave the Centre, bearing left around Meadley's Meadow and noting the particular points of interest. These include the section of iron fence that was erected in the 19th century to stop the villagers of Aldbury and Pitstone using the common to graze their animals (see article p.108).

The combination of this walk and the Woodland Trail (below) provides a perfect cameo of the beauty of the woods of the Chiltern Hills.

▶ From the Bridgewater Monument (erected in 1832 to the Duke of Bridgewater), follow the points of interest indicated by a burgundy-coloured ring and a number.

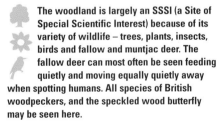

The woodland is largely an SSSI (a Site of Special Scientific Interest) because of its variety of wildlife – trees, plants, insects, birds and fallow and muntjac deer. The fallow deer can most often be seen feeding quietly and moving equally quietly away when spotting humans. All species of British woodpeckers, and the speckled wood butterfly may be seen here.

▶ The bridge over the sunken drovers' road from Pitstone was replaced in 1993 using sweet chestnut produced on the estate. It has been made accessible to people using manual and battery-powered vehicles – it is possible to borrow battery-cars from the Visitor Centre.

 WCs at Visitor Centre.

Right: The beech is the most important tree of the Chilterns.

Along the route is an example of enclosure – an earth bank dating from the early 1660s to protect Sallow Copse from animals grazing on Pitstone Common (see below and article p.108). Since grazing ceased on Pitstone Common in the 1920s, birch and scrub have invaded the common. Clinkmere Pond, a dewpond towards the end of this walk, was created to allow grazing animals to drink; frogs, newts and dragonflies may be found here and there is a pond-dipping platform for schoolchildren.

▶ Return to the car park or visitor centre to consider the next, larger, concentric walk.

The 2½-mile route around Old Copse and Thunderdell Wood is more strenuous, as it includes a steepish downhill and steady uphill climb.

▶ From the Visitor Centre, walk past the start of the Meadley's Meadow walk and on downhill towards Aldbury, along a section of the Boundary Trail.

Above: Green woodpecker

This is a good place to see butterflies, including the ringlet, one of our darkest species, and the slow-flying speckled wood. In recent years conservationists have recognised the value of fallen trees to many species of plants, birds and, above all, insects; here the National Trust has deliberately left wood on the ground.

▶ Head uphill (can be very muddy) and over the busy B4506, along a bridleway with the remains of a wood bank on the left.

This was another early attempt to enclose a wood, Thunderdell Wood, against grazing animals on Northchurch Common. The field on the right formed part of the medieval deer-park that supplied meat for Ashridge House (not NT, now a management centre); today's fallow deer are descendants of these animals.

▶ After passing the end of the field, the route is effectively straight ahead until the wide grassy path known as Princes Riding is reached. Turn left here, cross the road again and return along Monument Drive.

Other walks on the Estate

The Duncombe Terrace walk is different from all the others as it is a straight out and back route, partially hard-surfaced. Once again, it begins at the Visitor Centre, is particularly recommended for families and is suitable for push- and wheelchairs. The walk passes the site of a Roman Villa, a Bronze Age burial mound, and a copy of the Victorian Shooting Lodge, burnt down in 1989, which was originally used by shooting parties from Ashridge House.

Through the trees there are wonderful vistas and the many species of tree contribute to the story of the estate – for just one example on this route, look for the hazel coppices.

The three-mile walk around Ivinghoe Beacon is strenuous, including a couple of steep hill climbs. Starting from Step's Hill car park (grassed, not hard-standing), it passes through part of the Ivinghoe Hills Nature Reserve, a nationally important home to many plant (including orchids) and insect species, particularly butterflies, found only on chalk land. The mix of habitats also attracts many passage birds and in both spring and autumn wheatear and the blackbird-like ring ouzel pause here on their way to and from their more favoured haunts in northern England and Scotland.

Finally, for the really determined walker, there is the 16-mile Ashridge Estate Boundary Trail. Like all the others (except the Ivinghoe Beacon walk) it can begin at the Visitor Centre, although it can be joined at various points around the route. It begins with the Duncombe Terrace walk, passes Clipper Down and Crawley Wood, and traverses the Ivinghoe Hills Nature Reserve – the walk can be started here at Steps Hill car park on Beacon Road. After turning away from the Beacon, it skirts the villages of Ringshall (parking at Ling Ride car park) and Little

Gaddesden before passing along the Golden Valley and on to Frithsden.

 The Alford Arms.

The walk turns back towards Berkhamsted Common then, seemingly perversely, begins a long loop to Northchurch Common (parking nearby) swinging back to pass close by Aldbury.

The final section is uphill to the Monument, reversing the early part of the Old Copse walk.

Above: Bee orchid

57

GARDENS

Some of the walks in this book have gardens as a major feature – others pass tantalisingly close to tempting gardens. Here are some highlights.

Cliveden, overlooking the River Thames, has a series of gardens featuring roses, topiary, water, herbaceous borders and a parterre. The views across the river from the terrace are outstanding. (The garden is reached from Cookham.)

Hughenden Manor's high-Victorian-style garden was designed for Disraeli, whose wife Mary-Anne planned the terrace; her designs have helped the National Trust to restore the garden.

The 18th-century landscaped grounds at Osterley Park contain mature trees, including cedars, limes and liquidambars. Flowerbeds in the pleasure grounds have a wide variety of herbaceous plants chosen to ensure colour over a long season.

The garden at Fenton House is as unexpected as it is beautiful. Set on

Below: The geometric parterre at Cliveden

Hampstead Hill, it has been designed on two levels. The lower level contains the orchard and kitchen garden, and above this are the terrace walks, a lawn and flower borders. Recent additions have included a herb garden, scented border and sunken rose garden.

Ham House was once the home of Elizabeth Murray, who allowed the house to be used by Cromwell's troops in the Civil War. Seventeenth-century formality, in its parterres and terraces, and the strongly architectural nature of the wilderness, dominates the garden, which has been restored to its original design; the 17th-century kitchen garden is being restored at the time of writing.

The extensive Polesden Lacey estate includes a superb walled rose garden, a rock garden, lavender and iris gardens and herbaceous borders. There are sloping lawns and landscape walks with views of the house, and to Ranmore Common.

In Kent, three more gardens feature in two of the walks. Chartwell is where Sir Winston Churchill indulged a passion for designing his own garden, building walls and constructing a water garden, rose garden and a lake for his black swans. Emmetts is linked to Chartwell in our walk; it suffered greatly in the storm of 1987. Now a far more open landscape, dire predictions about the loss of the outstanding bluebell wood

proved wide of the mark – if anything they, and the daffodils, appear better, a wonderful sight every spring. This 19th-century garden has wonderful displays of shrubs, roses and a sunken rock garden. It would be a pity to leave Ightham Mote without seeing the surrounding garden, with lakes and woodland, an enclosed garden whose walls are adorned with clematis from spring onwards, and kitchen garden.

While on the Wandle Trail, it is worth having a look at Morden Hall Park for its superb rose garden, and The Grove at Carshalton, to admire its water features. Leith Hill has a splendid rhododendron garden. And when you are on the Thames Path, make time to visit Tradescant Garden and the Museum of Garden History in Lambeth, as well as the Temple Garden with its fountains and courtyards.

Above: Bay trees in pots and catmints at Fenton House

WALK 8

OSTERLEY PARK &
THE GRAND UNION CANAL

Map: OS 1:25,000 Explorer 161 London South

OS grid reference: TQ 146780

Distance: 7 miles, but see text

Terrain: Flat, easy, but care needed with exposed tree roots, particularly near lake, on first walk. Some pavement on second walk.

Getting there: By train – Syon Lane 1½ miles, Underground – Boston Manor, or Osterley (Piccadilly Line) turn L and L again ½ mile By bus – Hounslow/Hammersmith; Hounslow/Osterley to within ½ mile By car – off A4. Parking in Osterley car park

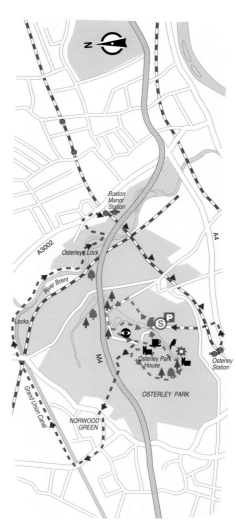

For convenience, both walks are described as beginning and ending in the visitor car park. They can be joined to provide a seven-mile route, or can be sampled separately. The first walk, 2½ miles, is based on the Estate Walk (leaflet available), and explores the park and pleasure gardens. The second walk is about 4½ miles (without the train journey) and allows the walker to sample the Grand Union Canal. For those on foot, an ideal day out might be to have lunch at Osterley, explore the house between the walks and complete the second walk at Boston Manor Underground.

Key

▬ ▬ ▬ Grand Union Canal Walk

▬ ▬ ▬ Osterley Circular Walk

Two circular walks starting and finishing at the car park

▶ Start the first walk at the gate in the corner of the visitor car park beside a small wood. Turn right along Nine Acre Path across farmland with grazing livestock, then sharp left into the wide Osterley Lane. Remarkably, the popular pedestrian area around the House and Garden Lake does not extend to this part of the walk. There are good views back to the house along this section, but passing by Middle Lake, the vistas of the house possess a classic beauty.

Originally built in 1565, the Tudor house was transformed by Robert Adam into a neo-classical villa at the behest of the owners of Child's Bank, who wished to use it to entertain friends and business contacts. The house is surrounded by some 145 hectares (360 acres) of park and farm land, and the peaceful atmosphere seems capable of absorbing at least some of the noise from both the M4 motorway, which borders the estate, and aircraft on the approach to Heathrow Airport.

▶ To avoid some of the traffic noise from the M4, go through the small wooden gate near where the lane turns left, parallel with the motorway, and enter the woodland area (point 20 on the Estate Walks leaflet). Here the path winds between oak, chestnut and sycamore planted in the 19th century.

For those with very limited time, a delightful walk is to leave the Estate Walk at point 19, continue beside the lake, rejoining the road from the house near to the car park.

Continue forward to a clearly defined junction, turn left and walk along a long avenue back to the house.

Glance back along the Elm Avenue, one of the original drives to the house (see second walk). Pass between the house and the stables, through a gate leading to the back of the house and some lovely views of the parkland to the north.

Below: The garden house at Osterley, designed by Robert Adam.

▶ Turn right along the path to the Garden House in the Pleasure Grounds – a beautiful 18th-century garden which supplies the house with plants and flowers, maintaining a fine show of colour even during normally fallow periods. The walk skirts the Arboretum and Pinetum (some magnificent cedar specimens) behind the Walled Garden, past the Orangery and behind the Temple of Pan, in front of which is a coast redwood, planted by the 7th Earl of Jersey. Here, the Outer Pleasure Ground walk begins, and follows the line of the old boundary ditch. The route is along a tarmac path which, although a little rough, is suitable for most walkers in most conditions and seasons. It progresses through a wooded area, with pine and other evergreens and a variety of bushes. It is possible to divert through the trees about halfway along on the left to have a view of the house, but do return the same way as the other paths do not lead back to the walk!

At the head of the Garden Lake there is a brick bridge known as the Boat House; steps beneath it led down to a boat used to take the family and guests out onto the lake. Here bulrushes grow in summer, and there are moorhen, duck, swan and the omnipresent Canada geese.

Below: The 'temple' portico of the East Front of Osterley Park

▶ Continue along the side of the lake (care with the tree root systems), returning either to visit the house, the Tudor stable block for refreshments or the car park. Much of the park is accessible to wheelchair users.

Refreshments, including meals, are available in the restaurant. Other visitor facilities include WCs.

The Grand Union Canal

▶ Walk up from the car park towards the house, with the lake on the left, passing the house and stable block – or start from the stables after refreshments! Go through a gate and along the Elm Avenue; at the end, turn left along Osterley Lane, crossing the bridge over the M4 motorway. Turn right onto the footpath which is signed to Norwood Green, crossing a field and passing through a narrow lane to St Mary's Avenue. Cross this road, and go through another narrow pathway to Tentelow Road. Take a a left past the church, and then take the first right-hand turn onto Norwood Green Road, along the edge of the green.

Turn right onto Norwood Road, cross the canal and turn right down the steps to the towpath onto the Grand Union Canal Walk. Follow this excellent path eastwards along the canal, passing the flight of eight locks comprising Hanwell Lock. This is a very pretty stretch, with narrow boats passing up and down and coot and moorhen always prominent.

After the last Hanwell Lock, notice the River Brent joining the canal from the left. The footpath crosses the river, and the path name changes here to the Brent River Park Walk. There are many wild flowers along this section, which passes a weir crossing to an islet in the river. Walk on to Osterley Lock, crossing a second bridge immediately before the motorway.

Below: Narrowboats on the Grand Union Canal at Osterley Lock

Turn left onto a wide track leading uphill to the entrance to playing fields; cross Southdown Avenue to Boston Road and turn right to Boston Manor Underground station. From here take a train one stop to Osterley Station, turning left onto the Great West Road (A4), and left again up Thornbury Road back to Osterley Park. Alternatively, it is possible to return to central London from either station.

Above: Gort and Saturn, Osterley Lock, Grand Union Canal

WALK 9

DEDHAM VALE

Map: Map: OS 1:25,000 Explorer 196 Sudbury, Hadleigh & Dedham Vale

OS grid reference: TM 077332 (Bridge Cottage)

Distance: 2½ miles via Dedham; 5½ miles via Stratford St Mary; 1½ miles from Manningtree

Terrain: Flat, easy walking. Can be very wet. Stout footwear required.

Getting there: By train – Manningtree 1½ miles by footpath. Bus: Ipswich/Colchester to E Bergholt ½ mile

By car – on N bank of Stour, 1 mile S of East Bergholt (B1070). (Car park charge, incl. NT members. Parking for disabled people near cottage; self-drive buggy available)

NB The walks may be started from several points – Flatford, Manningtree or Dedham.

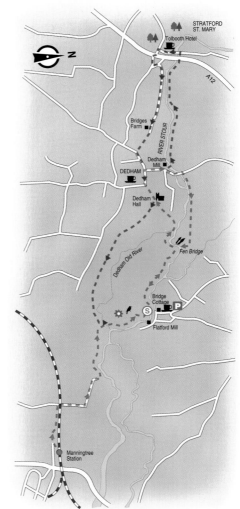

Within relatively easy reach of London, Colchester or Ipswich, this area of the peaceful Stour valley is something of a 'honey pot', as are the nearby villages of Dedham and East Bergholt. Flatford is at the centre of a number of walks, most associated with John Constable and some quite busy. Our suggestions take the walker away from the busiest areas, permitting a leisurely

Key

━ ━ ━ Extended Walk from Bridge Cottage

━ ━ ━ Bridge Cottage Circular Walk

introduction to the landscape that so absorbed the artist. The TIC sells maps and walks leaflets for the Stour Valley and Dedham Vale.

☕ **All-day refreshments at licensed tea-room where food is shared with some fearless sparrows!**

Two circular walks starting from Bridge Cottage

Park at car park, walk downhill to the cluster of buildings at Bridge Cottage. We suggest joining the popular circular route, an excellent introduction to the area, following the banks of the river Stour to the lovely village of Dedham.

Above: Cattle grazing beside the Stour

▶ Walk over the awkward bridge and cross the river from Suffolk into Essex, the first of several 'border crossings'. Take a well-trodden grass path (part of the St Edmund Way recreational path which reappears at various points along our walks) through the fields, passing peaceful scenes of grazing cattle, ducks and swans and people boating gingerly along. The river is lined with ancient oaks and pollarded willows.

✏️ **Near Fen Bridge is the site of Constable's painting _The Leaping Horse_.**

▶ Remain on the south of the river, entering Dedham along a narrow lane bordered by high hawthorn hedges, and then a metalled road fringed by houses, including Dedham Hall.

☕ **Restaurants and pubs (very busy at meal times).**

▶ Turn left, then right at Mill Lane, to Dedham Mill (no longer working and converted into apartments, but still attractive). Here there is an opportunity to take a further walk via Stratford St Mary (see below) or to return to Flatford.

Shortly beyond Dedham Mill, cross the river bridge (limited parking on left before the bridge), turning right through a kissing gate, past the boat-houses, into fields beside the river. Walk forward to Cradle Lane, a raised causeway through the water meadows that Constable used on his way to school from Flatford to Dedham. This narrow path is fringed with ancient oak trees and a canopy of tall bushes (poor surface, often wet, tree roots). At the T-junction it is possible to continue to the left along Fenbridge Lane and into East Bergholt, but the route is to the right, crossing Fen Bridge, then left to regain the path to Bridge Cottage.

▶ The extended walk leaves through a jumble of gates at Dedham Mill, crossing the river and clinging close to it as it meanders past a disused lock towards Stratford St Mary (to reach the village turn right at Stratford Bridge, under the A12).

The walk turns left along the road past the Tolbooth Hotel, and crosses above the A12. Take a sharp left, passing behind another hotel, joining the Essex Way and walking along the south side of the Stour back to Dedham past Bridges Farm (NT).

We recommend returning to Bridge Cottage by walking through Dedham to the sign-posted point of entry. Start towards Flatford but beyond Dedham Hall turn right, following the track, and later a footpath, near to the Dedham Old River, before bearing left to rejoin

Below: The river Stour at Dedham

the St Edmund Way near the barrage (see below). The path turns north, remarkably unfrequented. Only as the path widens on reaching Flatford Mill does it becomes populated by visitors photographing the famous view over the millpond.

> The path moves close to the river between reed beds, with whitethroat and other warblers present in summer, a variety of wild flowers and marsh plants and even an occasional orchid in the low vegetation.

▶ Visitors arriving at Manningtree Station by train or car may join the start of the St Edmund Way beside the car park (charge). The route is to the right along a farm lane (the 1½-mile route to Flatford is waymarked from the car park) and right again passing under the railway bridge. Follow the lane ahead then left for a second long section to a kissing gate. The route towards the Stour is

well defined – turn left at the river. From another kissing gate there is a view of Dedham church and the flood control, known as Judas Gap, is nearby. This is the place where tidal and freshwater sections of the river meet. A little farther on, turn north, linking with the path from Dedham. NB: The St Edmund Way passes along the concrete and metal barrage and care is needed negotiating this hazard and the steps at the end.

▶ Finally, there is a pleasant short walk from Bridge Cottage along the lane past the Mill, the Field Studies Centre and Willy Lott's Cottage – a favourite subject of Constable – then around Gibbonsgate Field (this short walk is level and suitable for wheelchair users).

Below: Bridge Cottage, Flatford

Right: The lock at
Dedham

Below: Willows on
the bank of the river
Stour

WALK 10

FINCHAMPSTEAD RIDGES & THE BLACKWATER VALLEY

Map: OS 1:25,000 Explorer 160 Windsor, Weybridge and Bracknell

OS grid reference: SU 822636

Distance: 7½ miles

Terrain: Mostly flat, uphill from Hall Farm to Finchampstead Ridges. Can be very muddy and uneven in the Ridges and, inevitably, wet along the Blackwater River section. Sensible, stout, footwear required at all seasons.

Getting there: By train – Crowthorne station
By bus – Henley-on Thames/Crowthorne, Wokingham/Finchampstead
By car – B3348 Crowthorne station & Finchampstead Ridges; unclassified road to Horseshoe Water Sports Centre.

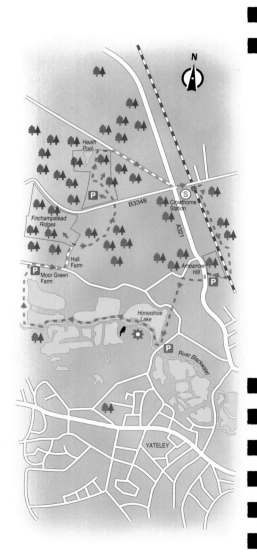

The walk has the advantage of being accessible at a number of different points: Crowthorne Station (car park charge, reduced rate after 10am), limited car parking at Ambarrow Hill, Horseshoe Water Sports Centre car park, Moor Green Farm car park and Finchampstead Ridges car park.

Although it is surrounded by increasingly built-up areas, including the villages of Sandhurst, Yateley and Crowthorne, and close to Camberley, Bagshot, Wokingham and Bracknell, this delightfully varied walk incorporates several small NT properties and a tranquil section of the Blackwater River. It passes through farm and woodland, and circumnavigates lakes and pools.

A circular walk starting and ending at Crowthorne Station car park

▶ From Crowthorne Station a public footpath leads south for about a third of a mile along the railway line until it reaches a wide, grassy area and a level crossing. Turn right up two or three steep steps and over

the crossing to Ambarrow Hill (NT), a wooded area worth exploring for the views from its pine-clad top.

The route is now along the Three Castles Path from Ambarrow Court Nature Reserve car park (care needed crossing the busy A321). Continue straight ahead to a small country lane; turn left almost immediately off this lane past Ambarrow Farm, following the path for about half a mile, latterly beside Horseshoe Lake.

At the lively Horseshoe Water Sports Centre, the easy-access Blackwater Valley Path turns out of

Below: Simons Wood

the car park, following the River Blackwater; there are several signed posts here, but the route is clear. Once away from the Sports Centre the walk, although well frequented, is peaceful and rural.

The Blackwater is a typical 'southern' river, here flowing serenely past gardens, water meadows and trailing willow branches while the prolific Himalayan balsam adds a splash of purple colour in summer. Look out for kingfisher, various duck, coot, moorhen and the inevitable Canada goose for most of the year, and listen for the delightful songs of several species of warbler in summer.

► Efforts are being made to upgrade the path to allow access on this section for wheelchair users. It already has one or two sections of boardwalk over some particularly marshy areas. Because of the path's popularity – part of it also serves as a bridleway – the surface can get churned up in damp conditions, but it is wide enough to make progress relatively straightforward.

About half-way along, there is a clearly marked footpath on the right (note, it is not shown on OS Explorer 160). This possible short cut, popular with locals, leads past the middle lake and returns to the Sports Centre.

At a bridge, the Three Castles Path turns sharply away, left, but continue along the path, narrower now, before turning right past the end of the existing lakes and ponds. Note that there are signs pointing forward at this point but the route is

to Moor Green Farm car park (another possible starting point). Tantalisingly visible through the trees for much of the walk, the lakes now stretch out on the right.

In summer, common tern can be seen diving for small fish in the nearest lake and they nest on an island here. Lapwing, swans, duck (particularly in winter), grebe, whitethroat, willow and reed warblers, as well as meadow brown and other species of butterfly, are all likely to be seen on this section of the walk.

►At the car park, turn right along the road for a few hundred yards, then left along the lane just before Hall Farm, leading to a short, steep and muddy walk up to the edge of Finchampstead Ridges (NT). A diversion into this wood and heather-clad slope, very typical of the area, allows views of Berkshire, Hampshire and Surrey. The walk turns right, up a path which crosses the B3348, known here as Wellingtonia Avenue, and into Simons Wood (NT). At this point, it is possible to turn right along the road (straight, but there is fast traffic) for about half a mile back to Crowthorne Station.

As Simons Wood and the adjoining Heath Pool (NT) are criss-crossed with paths from the car park, the best solution here may be to choose the least rutted and muddy route leading to Heath Pool. At the end of the Pool, there are crossroads. Turn right here and then, shortly, fork right along a straight lane – about a third of a mile – back

Above: Heath Pool, Simons Wood

to the roundabout on the junction of the A321 and the B3348. Negotiate the roundabout and return, in 100 yards or so, to Crowthorne Station.

Above: Mute swans' mating display

WALK 11

MALDON TO NORTHEY ISLAND

Map: OS 1:25,000 Explorer 183 Chelmsford &
The Rodings
OS grid reference: TL 872058 Northey Island
Distance: 5 miles
Terrain: Flat and exposed, can be muddy and
uneven; sensible clothing and footwear
required at all seasons.
Getting there: By train – to Chelmsford then
bus, or Colchester then bus
By bus – Chelmsford-Maldon (10 miles);
Colchester-Maldon (16 miles)
By car – A12 (Chelmsford by-pass) then
A414. Public car parks off High Street
(charge)
NB: To walk on Northey Island a permit must
be obtained at least a day beforehand from
the resident warden (tel. 01621 853142). The
island is cut off by tides daily for four or five
hours. As the sea wall and saltings are a
nature reserve, dogs are not allowed, and
visitors are asked to keep to the footpaths to
protect the environment from damage; in
addition, saltings can be very dangerous. The
causeway can be slippery. The walk around
the island is waymarked (leaflet available).

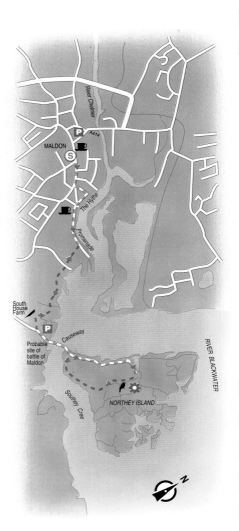

Right: Northey Island, looking towards the
estuary, at high tide.

This is a romantic, circular walk starting and ending in historic Maldon and visiting isolated Northey Island with its fascinating history and remarkable flora and fauna.

▶ Walk down to the Hythe – the Saxon word for wharf or landing place – from one of the car parks off the High Street. This busy quay is the centre of Maldon's thriving maritime industry, where several of the few surviving Thames barges (see article p.78) can be seen, moored at the quay or moving gracefully up and down the Blackwater. One of the regulars is 'Pudge' a veteran of the Dunkirk 'small ships' rescue.

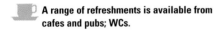

A range of refreshments is available from cafes and pubs; WCs.

▶ From the Hythe, walk southeast along the Blackwater, usually busy with river traffic moving between gleaming mudflats. On a beautiful summer day it is idyllic, but there isn't much high land between the

Above: Look out for curlew at low tide.

estuary and the Arctic so do be prepared for changeable weather.

Beyond Promenade Park the route passes various inlets and creeks, reaching the causeway to Northey Island (NT) in about a mile. The causeway is also accessible via a narrow lane, easily missed, between two houses on the Mundon Road. Beyond South House Farm is a small car park (for those only visiting Northey).

Close to the farm is where England's earliest battle was fought when, in AD991, the Vikings were raiding the eastern coast. After attacking Folkestone, Sandwich and Ipswich, they camped on Northey where Brihtnoth, Ealderman of Essex, confronted them. Anxious to achieve a decisive victory he permitted the Vikings to cross the causeway and was killed in the battle that followed – described in the epic poem, *The Battle of Maldon*.

▶ Walk over the causeway, believed to be of Roman origin, and a favourite with filmmakers requiring dramatic water crossings.

Partly due to its isolation, Northey Island attracts a wide variety of plants, birds and insects. Look out at low tide for oystercatcher, curlew and redshank on the mud, turnstone and rock pipit beside the causeway. Common tern are prominent in summer while heron stalk their prey at all seasons. Up to 5,000 over-wintering Brent geese feed on the fields to the east; in summer the fields are grazed by cattle to fertilise the grass in preparation for their arrival.

▶ The walk continues on the road, with farmland on the right – bounded by a variety of rather stunted trees (caused by the effect of salt and wind).

Blackthorn and rough grasses attract the Essex skipper butterfly and the handsome cream-spot tiger moth. Depending on the season, the bird hide on the left provides a sight of many waders and wildfowl; dunlin, black-tailed godwit, widgeon, shelduck and pintail all feed and roost on the island. Short-eared owls visit in winter.

▶ A little further on, the route turns right, but a brief diversion along the sea-wall leads to the wrecks of two Thames barges lying on the saltings. Return and continue around the island, following the path to the house of the donor family. The land beyond the picnic area is private, so continue along the sea-wall behind the house, turning right to walk beside a large expanse of high saltmarsh, flooded each month during the spring tides.

In early summer the pink flowers of thrift appear, followed by the mauve of sea lavender and, later, the yellow of sea aster; more colour is provided by the arrival in June of painted lady butterflies from North Africa. To the left a spur of the path leads out eastwards to Southey Creek, the best place in winter to watch birds like godwit, grey plover and red-breasted merganser; it is closed in spring to protect nesting birds.

▶ Continue and reach more saltings; normally, they act as a buffer defence against the sea but, by the late 1980s and for a number of reasons, they were disappearing. By way of an experiment, 100 yards of sea-wall were removed, a clay bank constructed to confine the water, and an entrance cut in it to enable the sea to flow through during one

Above: Thrift, in early summer

tide in every four. Silt was able to settle and generate a new saltmarsh. By mid-1992 marsh samphire and sea purslane were growing again on the higher ground and a year later samphire, known as the 'poor man's asparagus', had spread over much of the area. As a result of the experiment over twenty species of plants have now re-established themselves.

The route skirts a grass field on the right, with mature saltmarsh on the Southey Creek side, before passing through a kissing gate to rejoin the road to the causeway. Go over the causeway, turn right and return, beside the river, to Maldon.

77

THAMES BARGES

At the peak of their trading in 1860, there were 5,000 of these majestic barges. The premier cargo vessels for the best part of two centuries, they continued working until the 1960s. Today fewer than 40 remain. Some are still in daily use; some are house barges; others await restoration. They can be seen at various locations: the Thames, and from Snape Maltings in Suffolk to the River Medway in Kent.

The traditional Thames barges gradually evolved from the Middle

Ages and have changed little since the 17th century, although there were variations in design; spritsail rigged were Spritties; those with a square, overhung bowl were Swimmies, and Stackies were designed to transport straw and hay. The barges were built of oak, pitched pine or, in the later examples, steel, with sails that are traditionally dark chestnut red. They were designed to take large amounts of freight, while not compromising their stability, speed or ease of handling.

Thames barges draw less than four feet of water – a great advantage in the relatively shallow waters of the east coast of England. The hull has a flat, broad bottom that rests equally well in the sea, shallow water, or riverbed and, to accommodate rivers like the Thames, with its many bridges, they can lower their masts.

The barge was home to its skipper and crew, mostly two – 'a man, a boy and a dog', but sometimes a family, who all, including the children, had to pull their weight; bargees had to know how to cook, sew and do any necessary work on board, including carpentry.

The ability to carry out running repairs was vital if the barge was to

remain working, and competition for cargoes was fierce – an empty hold meant an empty pocket and empty stomachs. In addition, barge trading was the source of many shore jobs; a cargo of mud for a brickworks could take four men seven hours to load.

The depression of the 1930s led to a collapse from which the trade simply never recovered. Hundreds of barges were deserted and left to moulder at Woolwich and elsewhere on the Thames.

Some of the best remaining examples of Thames barges are regularly to be seen moored at the Hythe Quay at Maldon. Some have been set up as charitable trusts and are available for charter for cruises, for events such as weddings, and for educational purposes. The Thames Barge Sailing Club owns several of these fascinating vessels; two have been converted to accommodate up to fourteen people, and members of the club are responsible for their hire and maintenance. They sail with an experienced crew of skipper and mate, as in their hey-day, and one, 'Pudge', has her own place in history, for she

sailed to Dunkirk with other 'small ships' to take part in that miraculous evacuation on that dark day in 1940. Those who sail on her will see the plaque acknowledging her role.

Below: 'Pudge', distinguished veteran of Dunkirk.

WALK 12

DANBURY & LINGWOOD COMMONS

Map: OS 1:25,000 Explorer 183 Chelmsford &
The Rodings
OS grid reference: TL 783044 Danbury
Common; TL 784054 Lingwood Common
Distance: 5¹/₂ miles
Terrain: Mostly gentle slopes, some steeper.
Surfaces varied and, particularly in Blake's
Wood, can be very muddy and uneven. Stout
footwear recommended at all seasons.
Getting there: By train – to Chelmsford then
bus to the Bell Inn or Eve's Corner
By bus – Chelmsford/Maldon
By car – 5 miles E of Chelmsford, N & S of
A414

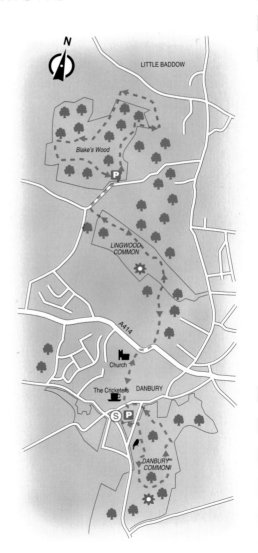

The Commons make up the second
largest area of common land in
Essex, the largest being Epping
Forest. The strategic value of the
Commons – set around one of the
highest hills in Essex and with views
to the Blackwater and Crouch valleys
– has been recognised for centuries.
An army camp was established here
in the 1780s to face a perceived
threat from the French Revolution
and it later formed part of the
defences raised in the early 19th
century, when a Napoleonic invasion

was expected. At least fourteen regiments were encamped on the Camp Ground to the south, and the area was used in both World Wars for training.

We propose a walk that links Danbury to Blake's Wood, over land with a fascinating history that also provides a microcosm of differing habitats. Broadly speaking, Danbury is open in character, Lingwood more heavily wooded, while Blake's Wood is a typical hornbeam and chestnut coppice. Our walk starts in Armoury car park, close to the timber-framed Armoury.

▶ Follow the trail across the road to find an example of the importance of areas of scrub for birdlife such as warblers, linnets and nightingales. To prevent the common reverting to the original forest, it is managed by cutting trees as they emerge. Walk south across the common to the Camp Ground – the boundary between the scrub and grass heathland – now the main car park and play area. From 1850 to 1900 cricket was played here; later it was used for village celebrations. As

Below: Lingwood Common is heavily wooded

traditional grazing and gorse cutting activities declined during the 20th century, the open aspect of the common began to disappear and thick stands of silver birch developed. Visually pleasing though birch bark may be, the trees are not of great value to wildlife and scrub and birch are being cleared, to encourage heather to regenerate.

The walk now enters an area of ancient woodland, needing minimum management but encouraging a wide diversity of trees, with felling to create glades and openings.

Random tree felling for fuel was practised by the Commoners when woodland returned to Danbury Common – coppiced trees can be seen in the wood (see p.108).

▶ Beyond the wood, walk through lowland heath where heather is being managed to simulate traditional cutting methods.

The dramatic decline in lowland heath everywhere over the last century has affected several vulnerable species, most significantly common lizard and adder. Shrubby alder buckthorn grows here, its autumn colours of yellow leaves and bright red berries a particular delight; the wood provides high-quality charcoal which, with saltpetre and sulphur, produces an even-burning fuse for explosives. It seems possible alder was deliberately introduced by the army.

▶ The route turns east then north, through an area of coppiced wood with some standard oaks. Soon the soil alters again from clay to sand and the vegetation reverts to silver birch and heather.

Here, a one-time grazing area, trees were pollarded 4–5 yards above the ground to protect the wood crop from livestock. The ground flora is richer here as regularly maintained pollards cast less shade and shed fewer leaves than other trees. Soldiers found this soil particularly suitable for vegetables – the area is still called 'Soldiers' Garden'.

▶ The walk moves into a damp area where some pipes and foundations are visible. This was the pumping station for an extensive water supply system that, in the late 19th century,

Above: Honeysuckle flower

supplied water to several local villages. Although the main spring was abandoned in 1936, the water flowing from it is said to retain its quality to this day.

At the lowest point of the Common, often flooded after heavy rain, a wet, boggy area has been created by introducing a series of dams. Snipe and woodcock can be seen in winter, newts in spring, and wetland flowers prosper here. After walking uphill, the final part of the walk is a hay meadow where about 40 species of wild flower have been recorded. Lesser calamint, now a rarity in Essex, grows here and can, superficially, be confused with pennyroyal; the road running parallel with the walk is known as Penny Royal.

Refreshments are available at The Cricketers.

► A footpath leads to Lingwood Common from near the pub, passing the playing fields and Danbury Church. Take a short right fork here, then right again at the A414 before shortly turning left, continuing north by a footpath through Bellhill Wood and onto the Common.

Heather (ling) does grow on open spaces on the slopes, but Lingwood is also wooded, with birch, oak and grassy glades, the haunts of butterflies and moths.

Right: Snipe can be seen here in winter

On Beacon Hill, the highest point and worth visiting for its views north to the Chelmer Valley, Neolithic flints have been found. Walk northeast across the common, turning right at the road and enter Blake's Wood at the car park, some 300 yards on the left.

Blake's Wood is 40 hectares (100 acres) of mixed woodland, with hornbeam and chestnut coppice (ancient and modern!), celebrated in spring for its show of bluebells and wood anemones. A $1\frac{1}{2}$-mile circular waymarked walk (Wildside Walk) has been created, starting at the car park and following the perimeter of the wood. This route can be very wet, even in summer.

Return to Danbury by the same route – perhaps exploring a little more of Lingwood.

WALK 13

LEITH HILL

Map: OS 1:25,000 Explorer 146 Dorking, Box Hill & Reigate

OS grid reference: TQ 139428 Abinger Road car park

Distance: 4^1/$_2$ miles including Rhododendron Wood

Terrain: Hilly, but not excessively so. Can be very muddy, damp and uneven in places. Stout footwear required at all seasons.

Getting there: By car – 1 mile SW of Coldharbour off A29/B2126

By train – Holmwood Station 2^1/$_2$ miles (not Sun), Dorking 5^1/$_2$ miles

No nearby bus services

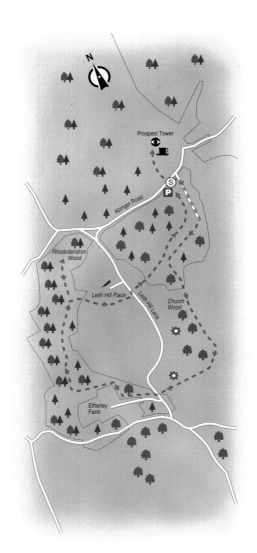

The views from the summit of Leith Hill alone justify the steep climb, but the property has much more to offer. Areas of deep wood and open fields (some being returned to hay meadows) provide a delightful contrast and a diversion to the Rhododendron Wood is strongly recommended (almost a necessity if you are visiting in spring or early summer!).

A circular walk from Abinger Road car park

The NT has two walks around Leith Hill (leaflet available); our walk covers part of the Orange Trail but continues south on a newly developed trail. From the Tower, return downhill following the waymarks over Abinger Road (or walk east from the car park to join the trail) and along a track to near Post 3 on the Orange Trail. Here the new route begins.

▶ We suggest you begin by making the half-mile climb to the summit of Leith Hill.

❋ This is the most arduous part of the walk but, from the top of the 18th-century Gothic Prospect Tower, 1,000 feet above sea level, there are marvellous views all round; to London, across the Weald, the South Downs and to the English Channel 26 miles to the south.
☕ The Tower houses exhibitions, information and a servery.

▶ Turn sharp left down the hill, along a wide, well-surfaced roadway fringed with trees, shrubs, and plants such as the bright purple self-heal and rosebay willowherb. About 150 yards along, the route leaves the wide track, branching right, and continuing along a grass path (often wet).

❋ Burdock can be found growing under the trees and enchanter's nightshade in the hedgerows. This is Church Wood, notable for its bluebells in spring. Soon the route is through an area still regularly coppiced, the various stages clearly visible.

▶ After crossing a lane, go over a stile and bear sharp left along the edge of an open field. A mown strip will help to identify the route as it skirts several open fields.

❋ These fields are being returned to hay meadow and will be grazed by stock at certain times to encourage the reappearance of wild flowers such as bugle and archangel. The hedgerows have a mixture of wild flowers, among them bird's foot trefoil and vetches.

▶ Crossing Leith Hill Lane, the route continues up the lane for about 50 yards, to a stile beyond the entrance to Etherley Farm. Turn left into another field with a good view up Leith Hill, and shortly back into

Above: There are marvellous views from the top of the 18th-century Tower.

woodland, along a lane leading to a wide bridleway. Climb uphill quite steeply, past a brackish pond on the right – in summer the pink-flowered centaury is common here.

At a T-junction the path rejoins the Orange route, offering several choices; we suggest a detour to the left following the waymarks to the Rhododendron Wood, a mass of colour in April and May, but still a delight through most of the summer. It is possible to follow the Orange Trail from here to the Tower but our walk retraces the route to the T-junction, going forward towards Leith Hill Place.

Leith Hill Place was the childhood home of the composer Ralph Vaughan Williams, who gave the house to the NT in 1945.

▶ For those who do not intend to visit the Wood, turn right at the T-junction. This route is through rough pasture, once parkland, with mature trees including an 250-year-old oak and good views of the house. Returning to Leith Hill Lane, turn left for about 25 yards, and look for a ramp on the right leading to a narrow path heading downhill. This path follows the wall, and newer fence, of a walled garden, becoming steeper, with tree roots forming a short flight of steps.

Right: A beech tree by the footpath at Leith Hill

There follows a short climb, past a pond on the right with a seat beside it. Then into an area of tall trees – Douglas fir and Norway spruce – before rejoining the Orange route at point 3 to return uphill to the car park.

Right: The Rhododendron Wood in Leith Hill Place

Below: The view from Leith Hill, in autumn

WALK 14

RIVER WEY NAVIGATION

Map: OS 1:25,000 Explorer 145 Guildford & Farnham

OS grid reference: SU 993502 (Dapdune Wharf)

Distance: 9 miles

Terrain: Mostly flat, along towpath, but some slopes. Surface reasonable with a few difficult stretches. Some tarmac/metalled surfaces. Can be muddy and slippery. Sensible footwear advisable at all seasons.

Getting there: By car – on Wharf Road, behind Surrey County Cricket Ground off A322 (Woodbridge Road), Guildford. By train – Guildford (for stations near other parts of Navigation, see NT Handbook). By bus – regular services in town

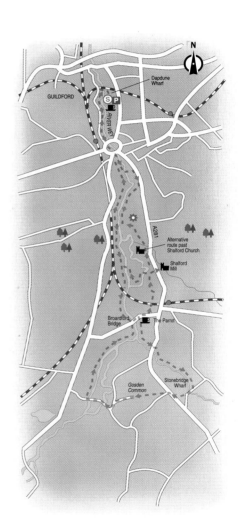

The National Trust has developed Dapdune Wharf using displays and exhibitions (including a barge) to provide a fascinating history of the Wey Navigation.

A circular walk from Dapdune Wharf car park

This 15½-mile waterway has linked Guildford with London, via Weybridge, since the mid-17th century. One of the first British rivers to be made navigable, it opened to barge traffic in 1653 and operated until the 1950s. With the opening of the Godalming Navigation a century later, a further four miles became available upstream.

 There is a small servery, normally open as wharf.
Adapted WCs.

▶ Leave Dapdune Wharf by turning right to the railway embankment. Cross the river (we deliberately refer to the 'river' but much of the walk is beside 'the navigation') by footbridge, turning back along the towpath, past the wharf. Walk under the road bridge, past the market and Town Bridge. Continue past the Britannia Inn and cross to the Yvonne Arnaud Theatre on the other side of the river.

Refreshments, including full meals, are available here.

Below: A traditional colourful narrowboat name-plate

▶ Turn right along Millmead Road, past the car park and the Wey Inn (previously The Jolly Farmer). After the iron bridge over the river, pass the rowing club, turning right (ignore the stile ahead of you) along a narrow lane at the back of the club building and through a gate. Follow a narrow tree-lined path by the water's edge, with Shalford water meadows on the left. Still close to the edge of the town, this is a peaceful and attractive part of the river, grazed by cattle. The way is fairly rough, in contrast to the broad towpath opposite; it is, of course, possible to stay on this path from the Britannia Inn.

A patch of woodland leads to the junction of the North Downs Way.

Rosebay willowherb, Himalayan balsam and meadowsweet predominate along the route in midsummer, following cow parsley and purple loosestrife.

▶ Turn right, crossing the river by the ugly footbridge at the foot of St Catherine's Hill and continue along the west side of the river, past a landslip. The sandy soil here is very unstable and care is needed as the landslip has a pronounced slope.

Take the towpath past St Catherine's Lock and the charming cottage on the opposite bank, and under two railway bridges. A National Trust sign, near a 1940s pillbox, indicates an extra loop to Broadford. Our route follows the towpath directly to Broadford Bridge, turning left over the bridge.

Here our suggestion is to continue to Stonebridge Wharf and Unstead Lock (both NT) before returning to Broadford – some three miles. (For a shorter walk see below.)

Over the bridge, turn immediately to the river and, following the waymarks for the Greensand Way, walk to Stonebridge Wharf, with its restored gunpowder store. Take the metalled road past the cottages and climb a stile – nearby is the short-lived Wey and Arun canal, opened in 1816 but closed by 1871; work over many years is succeeding in restoring sections.

At the main road turn right, cross the bridges, and go left again to join the disused railway track for a while. Under an arched bridge turn left, then right over the bridge and ahead to Horsham Road. Follow a path across the edge of Gosden Common, passing a sewage works before joining a metalled road. Bear left and right on this, crossing the river and the navigation, and turn right onto the towpath. Return to Broadford Bridge via the rebuilt Unstead Lock (NT).

Below: Sunlight on narrowboats on a frosty morning

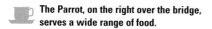

The Parrot, on the right over the bridge, serves a wide range of food.

▶ At Broadford, cross the road near the public house, walk ahead through a small car park, along a lane bordered at first by cottages, then through woodland up a slight rise. Where paths meet behind a pub car park, divert to the right, walking back a few yards along the A281 to visit Shalford Mill.

Shalford Mill, dating from the 18th century, was given to the NT in 1932 by a group of benefactors calling themselves Ferguson's Gang.

▶ Return to the route, go through a kissing gate (or see below), along a boardwalk, past the cottage, and

cross the river at St Catherine's Lock, retracing footsteps from there to the landslip and bridge. Remain on this bank with a further short diversion up St Catherine's Hill to the remains of the 14th-century chapel with good views of the town and valley. Return and follow the path into the town, passing cottages, houses and flats with delightful gardens; walk over the small islands by the theatre to Millbank car park or follow the route back to Dapdune Wharf.

▶ A marginally easier route from the rise is to take the track signposted to Guildford, passing Shalford Church and crossing Shalford Park, a large expanse of grassland.

Continue to Guildford on a metal track, returning to the A281 beside the rowing club, or turn left at the North Downs Way as it crosses the middle of the park. Follow it to the footbridge, before turning right for Guildford and Dapdune.

Above: The towpath beside the River Wey Navigations

Right: Shalford Mill, showing the brick water entry arches

WALK 15

KEW TO TEDDINGTON LOCK VIA HAM

Map: OS 1:25,000 Explorer 161 London South

OS grid reference: TQ 190778 to TQ 172732

Distance: 6½ miles

Terrain: Flat, easy, some pavement, towpath can be wet, if not flooded, so it is not always possible to walk along riverside in winter. The route is well waymarked along the Thames.

Getting there: By train – Kew Bridge Station, Kew Underground station

By bus – several possible

By car – A205 (South/North Circular Road)

Very restricted parking in Kew Green area

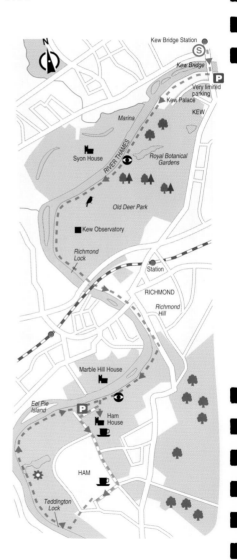

There are many choices of walk along the river, but this section of the Thames long-distance path provides some of the best views and is accessible from Kew, Richmond or Ham. It can be reached by Underground or bus, or by train to Kew Bridge Station on the north side of the river. The recommended route is from Kew, passing Kew Palace and the Royal Botanic Gardens. It continues past Old Deer Park and Richmond to Ham House and can be extended to include Teddington Lock and Eel Pie Island, returning to Ham (which is open from spring to autumn in the afternoon, five days a week – see annual NT Handbook or website for details.

A linear walk from Kew Bridge to Ham House

▶ If you are starting from Kew Bridge Station, cross Kew Bridge on the right-hand side, go down the steps immediately by the river on the west side, walk back to the river and turn left to follow the Thames Path through Kew and Richmond to Ham, and finally to Teddington Lock.

The route passes Kew Gardens on the left, from where there are views of a marina, just before Syon House appears across the river.

On the site of a medieval abbey, Syon House was built for the Duke of Northumberland in the 1760s, with interiors designed by Robert Adam.

The Path turns due south, past Isleworth and the island of Isleworth Ait on the right, and on the left Old Deer Park, a name familiar to most rugby players (at Isleworth there is a foot ferry giving access to Isleworth station, another possible starting point for the walk). Past Kew Observatory, continue southeast towards Richmond, past houseboats and various river craft from canoes to pleasure boats.

Right: Eel Pie Island

Birds frequently seen on the river include heron, grebe, duck, geese, and cormorant, which is increasingly common a long way upstream on the Thames.

▶ Pass the barrage at Richmond Lock, and continue along the Thames Path. Look back at times towards the top of Richmond Hill, dominated by the Star and Garter Home, famous for its care of long-stay servicemen from all theatres of war. Now the river begins to curve west and from here there is a splendid view of the superb Palladian Marble Hill House on the opposite bank (it is possible to make a detour to the house using the foot/cycle ferry).

Marble Hill House was built for George II's mistress, Henrietta Howard, Countess of Suffolk.

▶ A short way further along the south bank, the equally magnificent 17th-century Ham House appears through the trees, set back from the river. It is possible to divert to the house at this point, or continue to the large public car park by the river.

For visitors intending to park a car here, perhaps to take only the short circular walk (below), caution has to be the watchword – the park is liable to flooding during the winter, in very wet weather, or at particularly high tides.

From here, the circular route through Ham village connects with the Thames Path again at Teddington Lock and can be tackled in either direction. The suggested route is out of the car park, passing the pedestrian road to Ham House, continuing along Ham Common Road and through Ham Street, past some very pretty cottages and houses, some doubtless built for artisans, but all now highly prized.

There are several attractive inns on, or close by, the route. All serve food.

▶ Turn to the right at the crossroads by Ham Common, along Lock Road. The route continues over Broughton Avenue to Hardwicke Road, where it turns right for a very short distance; then left to cross Riverside Drive and

Right: The Cherry Garden at Ham House, with the marble statue of Bacchus.

on along a hardened path through woodland to the Thames, just past Teddington Lock – in reality three locks, the earliest dating from 1811.

This is the point at which the Thames ceases to be tidal, and about 250 yards below the lock there is an obelisk, marking the point at which control of the river passes from the Port of London Authority (downstream) to the National Rivers Authority (upstream). Teddington Lock Bridge links the Surrey and Middlesex sides of the river; from it the Weir, a very popular place with coarse fishing enthusiasts, can be seen.

▶ Turn right again past the busy lock. On the right are Ham Riverside Lands, open areas made with rubble

from London's bombsites after the Second World War. Parts of the path are inclined to be bumpy with puddles in poor weather, but it is popular with cyclists, walkers and joggers. Most of the walk is through trees, which provide welcome shade on hot days and some shelter in cold weather.

In summer, purple loosestrife, rosebay willowherb and Indian balsam flower are in profusion along the water's edge.

Right: The formal lavender beds, with box edging and yew hedges, at the east end of Ham House.

Above: Teddington Lock

▶Cross a bridge over an inlet where boats are moored on the right, and there are lovely river views on the left. The path, no more than five or six yards from the river, continues past Eel Pie Island, with its boathouses and eclectic dwellings – well known for 'raves' in the 'swinging 60s'– before emerging by the large free car park at Ham.

Lunches and teas are available in the Orangery Restaurant at Ham House, using produce from the kitchen garden, after which a visit to the house, a unique survival of 17th-century fashion, is recommended, combined with a period of relaxation in the restored formal garden. WCs.

WALK 16

ANKERWYCKE & WRAYSBURY

Map: OS 1:25,000 Explorer 160 Windsor, Weybridge and Bracknell
OS grid reference: TQ 006731
Distance: 4¹/₂ miles
Terrain: Flat, the Thames-side section can be muddy, sometimes impassable. A long section is on public roads but waterproof footwear is advisable in most seasons.
Getting there: By train – Wraysbury Station By car – M25 J12/13, signed to Wraysbury Ankerwycke Farm is off B376, approx 1 mile, left

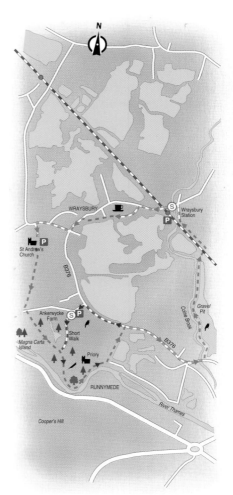

Although under the flight paths for Heathrow, Ankerwycke manages to project an impression of calm. Unspoilt, it offers a fascinating glimpse into English history and, now under the stewardship of the National Trust, will continue to do so, regardless of what happens to plans for the expansion of the airport.

Key

▬ ▬ ▬ Ankerwycke Farm Walk
▬ ▬ ▬ Wraysbury Station Walk

A circular walk starting and ending at Wraysbury Station car park

Park at Wraysbury Station (limited, but no charge) and turn left towards Wraysbury.

☕ **Refreshments available at two pubs in the village.**

▶ At Tithe Farm Cottages, turn left along Tithe Lane and follow the footpath past the edge of the lake, returning to the centre of the village (it is possible to remain on the road into the village). Turn right to St Andrew's Church (Victorian on a 13th-century site) and go through the churchyard into the meadows behind the church. There is access past the small stile into the first field, which has a fenced path through the centre; horses often graze in the pasture here. Two more stiles lead into a large meadow beyond the tarmac road (left here for a short cut to Ankerwycke Farm), with an unfenced path through its centre. It is possible to go left and right here to reach the Thames more quickly, then past Magna Carta Island, diverting left to visit the priory ruins and the yew. Follow the National Trust's way-

Below: Ankerwycke Farm

marked path through further meadows, leading to the ruined priory and the celebrated yew tree, then on to the banks of the Thames.

Surrounded by myths, the Ankerwycke yew is variously estimated to be between 2,000 and 2,500 years old and, it has been suggested, may be where King John was forced to sign Magna Carta in 1215 (a more usual choice is Magna Carta Island a little way back along the river – no one really knows!). With a girth of 9.5 metres (31 feet), the tree is still physically impressive and has a presence enhanced by the possibility that it is at least as old as Christianity.

As to the priory, it was founded in the reign of Henry II for Benedictine nuns. This is one of the many places where Henry VIII is alleged to have met Anne Boleyn clandestinely, although the priory was probably already a ruin. Today a small part of a wall is all that remains; of Ankerwycke House, the mansion built here, nothing survives. The parish of Wraysbury was enclosed (see article p.108) in 1799.

Jerome K. Jerome was clearly impressed by this area, mentioning the priory, Magna Carta Island and Henry and Anne in *Three Men in a Boat*. His description of courting couples is as true today as when written in 1889!

Ankerwycke has an interesting natural history – there are frequent sightings of rose-ringed parakeets, which are increasing in numbers and seem to enjoy this area. More exciting is the prospect of seeing short-eared owls in winter and hobbies in summer. When you reach the riverbank, look out for one of the several pairs of kingfishers living along this stretch of the Thames.

▶ At the river, turn left – the woodland route is somewhat uneven and muddy in wet weather, but the views are worth the effort, with a great variety of craft passing up and down the river. Here, the walker might well be in deepest countryside, were it not for the car parks and lawns of the Runnymede Pleasure Ground across the river. In summer, wild clematis wreathes around the trees, and there are many woodland flowers and plants, including lords and ladies with its bright orange fruits. Follow the path to a high brick wall; turn sharp left away from the river, past some private land with ponds on the right and farmland on the left. The route emerges onto the busy B376. At this point, it is possible to turn left along the road, returning in approximately half a mile to a road on the left leading to Ankerwycke Farm.

Above: Rose-ringed parakeets are increasing in number and seem to enjoy the area.

The route we suggest is to the right, using the verge, for about three-quarters of a mile, then left over the Colne Brook and onto a footpath which runs between the Brooke and a gravel pit.

🐦 **This lake, in common with the many other pits and reservoirs in the area, attracts large numbers of ducks during the winter, including pochard, goosander and goldeneye.**

▶ Go forward for about a mile, cross the railway line, then walk along the bridleway beside the line. On reaching the B376 again, turn left to return in a few yards to Wraysbury Station (no pavement), pausing to note the delightful cluster of houses along the Colne Brook.

A shorter walk, beginning at Ankerwycke Farm

▶ Go through a small kissing gate level with the farm buildings – still in use by the local farmer – and across a field, past some private houses on the left and a pond, usually with swans, on the right. There are fine views of Cooper's Hill and the Air Forces Memorial, high above Runnymede, on this walk. Follow the signs to the left and at an avenue of trees, probably once the drive between farm and priory, turn right towards the river, with the priory ruins on the right, and the ancient yew on the left. Thereafter, follow the route above, taking the left-hand option at the B376. (For those arriving by car, and not wishing to use the public roads, we suggest this walk, linked with a visit to Runnymede across the Thames – see Walk 2 on pp.22–26.)

This walk covers very similar ground to one of the excellent walks produced by the Colne Valley Park Groundwork Trust.

Below: Ankerwycke Lake

WALK 17

MANOR OF COOKHAM & MAIDENHEAD

Map: OS 1:25,000 Explorer 172 Chiltern Hills East

OS grid reference: SU 855815 (walk 1); SU 894853 (walk 2)

Distance: 7½ miles in total, both approx 3½ miles

Terrain: Mostly flat, easy, can be wet, particularly on second walk

Getting there: By train – Maidenhead, Bourne End

By bus – for information on public transport in Bucks 0870 608 2608

By road – A404 (M) Jct. 9b signed (on roundabout) Pinkneys Green

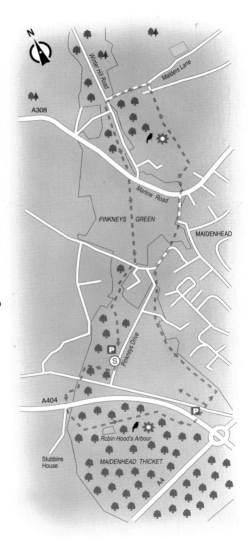

Significant areas of common land to the west and north of Maidenhead were bought by local residents and given to the National Trust in 1934. It's worth pointing out that the whole of the area is criss-crossed with paths and small patches of open common on which it is possible to roam almost at will; our suggestions can be readily adapted. The first of two walks visits the area closest to Maidenhead, including a small nature reserve (which can be a self-contained walk of ½ mile). The second is in and around the beautiful village of Cookham. It is possible to link the two walks on foot but we suggest they be treated separately – perhaps connected by lunch at one of the many pubs in the area.

A circular walk starting and ending at Pinkneys Drive car park

▶ A footpath at the edge of the car park leads north to a broad green ride, bordered by farmland (popular with riders, this area can be very muddy). Continue under a bridge carrying the A404 then climb some steps, follow the footpath and enter Maidenhead Thicket by the lodge of Stubbins House.

Turn east on an unmade, wide road, once the drive to Stubbins House, bordered by mature limes and sycamores, and some good horse chestnut trees.

The NT may introduce oak here as the limes die. It is a lovely walk in most seasons, with massed bluebells and primroses in spring. On the right is a clearing – Robin Hood's Arbour, a Belgic farm enclosure – with a range of flowers, including orchids. In spring and summer, birdsong vies with the noise of traffic, inevitably a problem although, to balance the noise, the paths are almost deserted.

Right: A view of the river Thames from the garden at Cliveden

▶ The path narrows and then turns left, crossing a narrow pedestrian bridge over the beginning of the A404 (M) link road. Ahead, through an NT car park, is a wide area of meadow, full of common flowers. Wander at will over this meadowland, but a turn to the left through or around the meadow will bring you back to Pinkneys Green car park.

For a longer walk, proceed across the meadow to the village of Pinkneys Green, taking care on the road northeast through the village. At the junction of the A308 Marlow Road, join a footpath, bearing right past Pinkneys Farm. Take the first fork, due north, to Malders Lane, beside the Old Brick Works site.

Now a tiny and inspired nature reserve, this former site of a brick and tile works was acquired by the NT in 1989. The warden recognised the potential of this site with its ponds, woodland and clearings, and created a nature walk which is accessible to everyone, including wheelchair users and people with impaired vision – there are tapping rails, observation platforms by the ponds, and a variety of wildlife to enjoy (limited parking in Malders Lane for those wishing to start from the reserve).

▶ On leaving the reserve, turn left along the tarmac lane and left again at the main road (Winter Hill Road). Walk south, on the common land, back towards Pinkneys Green. On the west edge of the village a footpath skirts the buildings. Fork left in a few yards, returning to the car park.

Cookham Village and the Thames, via Winter Hill

If arriving by car, park in Cookham Moor car park (NT) at the west edge of Cookham village.

There is a choice of places to eat here and at Cookham Dean; restaurants and pubs including the Bel and the Dragon.

▶ Walk across the green into the village, enjoying the well-maintained red brick and white-painted cottages

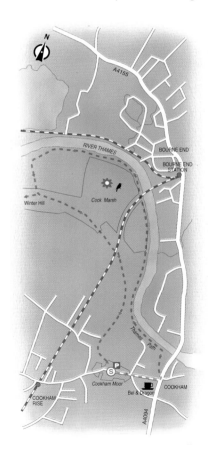

and houses before turning north at the road junction in order to join the waymarked Thames Path at the utterly delightful approach to the church. Pass through the churchyard and the route is left, initially on a tarmac path, along the west bank of the river. A lot of craft moor here, while the other bank is crowded with river-front properties.

The route continues past Cock Marsh (NT) on the left. At the railway bridge, the Thames Path changes banks, heading to Bourne End (a possible starting point for this walk is Bourne End station), but continue forward along the bank as the river makes a wide sweep left.

About half a mile further on, the footpath leaves the river, heading

inland to enter Cock Marsh just below the steep escarpment.

▶ A right turn here will lead eventually to another NT property – Winter Hill – but the walk continues left, under the escarpment, and bearing gently right, returns in approximately 1¹/₂ miles to the car park.

Above: Woodland at Maidenhead and Cookham Commons

The marsh, grazed as common land since 1272, and still grazed by commoners' cattle, is remarkably undisturbed and supports a wide variety of bird and plant life; the Trust considers it to be among the best wetland sites it owns for breeding waders.

Cliveden (NT – house, restricted opening) is across the river from Cookham and is only accessible to walkers along busy public roads. The extent of the features in the extensive grounds, including a remarkable Victorian fountain, water and rose gardens, a formal parterre best seen from the terrace of the house, and magnificent hanging woods, delightful walks by the Thames and superb views, make any visit, at every season, a joy. There can be few greater contrasts than to proceed here after a day spent in the Manor of Cookham.

Above: Cookham Church

 Refreshments and WCs.

COMMON LAND

Few areas of England are without a common, or a relic of one, survivors of a system of husbandry dating back over a thousand years. For most of that period, commoners were permitted to graze livestock on local commons or manorial waste – scrub, woodland, heath, fenland or moor, often at some distance from the village. 'Common' is something of a misnomer as land is always owned, whether by individuals, often 'the lord of the manor' or,

these days, public bodies including the National Trust. 'Commoners rights' are an entitlement to use certain clearly defined rights over the land. The main categories of rights are ancient rights, usually quite specific, and the less tangible rights, to air, light and recreation.

Although other ancient rights do exist, the five most widespread were those of pasture, estover, turbary, piscary and right in the soil. The right of pasture is the important right to graze livestock. Equally valuable was estover, the right to cut and take wood, reeds, heather, and bracken; turbary granted rights to dig turf or peat. The right of piscary permitted the taking of fish from ponds and streams; and in the soil, the right to take sand, gravel, stone, coal and minerals. These rights were first defined in the Middle Ages, with limitations as to quantities and season.

For centuries, landowners tried to take control of the land by enclosing it, but it was not until the late 18th and 19th centuries, when enclosure was supported by measures in Parliament, that the system came under sustained pressure.

Above: Horsell Common, near Woking

The National Trust owns a great deal of common land, including a significant amount around London; the following examples give a brief glimpse of aspects of the history of those commons.

On Danbury Common villagers cut gorse and bracken for animal litter and compost, dug and dried turfs for fuel. This impoverished the soil, encouraging heather which had various uses, including thatching. Scrub then developed, to be replaced by trees, which were felled for fuel. The cut trees produced multiple stems and these coppiced trees were harvested to provide more wood.

The commons at Frensham, Milford and Witley are now managed for the benefit of wildlife; heather and gorse are grown specifically to encourage certain species while the commoners treated both as commodities; heather for thatching and broom-making, gorse for animal fodder and fuel. Treating gorse as a food source for insects and to encourage birds like the stonechat and Dartford warbler is a very modern concept.

As the traditional uses of the commons steadily declined, many were used for recreational purposes such as cricket, golf and horse-riding. Many commons became 'lungs' for those in urban areas. Around London there are, in addition to commons, public 'forests' (Epping and Hatfield)

Above: Silver birches on Horsell Common

and long-established Royal Parks. The new 'rights' associated with walkers, cyclists and riders are staunchly guarded by these successors to the commoners.

Above: Trees and heather on Frensham Common

WALK 18

FRENSHAM COMMON

Map: OS 1:25,000 Explorer 133 Haslemere
& Petersfield/145 Guildford & Farnham
OS grid reference: SU 845404 Frensham
Great Pond car park; SU 858417 Frensham
Little Pond car park
Distance: 4½ miles (King's Ridge Walk)
Terrain: Sandy, uneven, mostly unmade
paths. Can be wet. Sensible, stout, footwear
required at all seasons.
Getting there: By train – Farnham
By bus – Farnham/Hindhead/Haslemere
By car – A287 Hindhead-Farnham road)

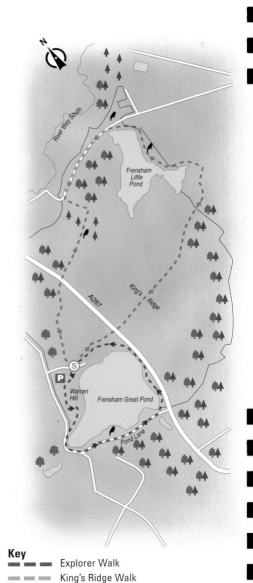

This area of common land, lakes (the
Ponds) and a nature reserve is not
only important for the remarkable
mix of wildlife species – including
rarities – but is also a significant
recreational centre for many visitors.

Waverley District Council, who
share the management of the site
with the Trust, has created a cycle
trail over some 4½ miles of track.
There are four self-guided walks
(leaflet available). We have combined
parts of three of the walks to provide
a route that includes both Ponds and
a range of habitat. Do note that large

Right: Trees and heather on Frensham Common

Key
▬ ▬ ▬ Explorer Walk
▬▬ ▬▬ ▬▬ King's Ridge Walk

areas of the Common to the south, including the hills known as the Devils Jumps, can also be explored on foot.

Figure-of-eight walk from the Great Pond Information Room car park (King's Ridge Walk)

Both Frensham's ponds were created in the Middle Ages to supply fish to the Bishop of Winchester's estate. The Great Pond was drained in the Second World War, to prevent enemy aircraft using it as a landmark.

▶ Starting from the car park, walk east to find and follow the orange waymarks (the blue signs seen on the walk indicate bridleways). With the Pond to the right, walk towards, and cross, the A287 and up to King's Ridge, so named because King Edward VII once reviewed troops from it.

Note the humps on the ridge – Bronze Age burial mounds. Beyond the ridge there is a chance that stonechats will be seen, perched on the gorse. The Dartford Warbler has been making a comeback in recent years – it now appears at sites well into East Anglia.

▶ The route circles Vampire Flats, the site of a Vampire aircraft crash in 1948, and leads to a causeway through an area of wet woodland. Mostly alder, this is a winter home for redpoll and siskin. Walk round the Little Pond, in part a wildlife sanctuary.

Below: A swan glides across Frensham Little Pond

Frensham Ponds seem always to attract rarities; the naturalist, Gilbert White received one of five black-winged stilt shot by the pond keeper in 1779. Migrating osprey regularly appear perhaps attracted by the alleged similarity of the Scots pine woodland to their breeding grounds – filmmakers who do not wish to travel as far as Scotland apparently use the site!

▶ The route now turns west, zig-zagging across areas of birch and pine scrub, regularly cleared to maintain the heathland habitats. Beyond the A287 is an area of exposed sandy soil.

This site is valuable for supporting rare insects and reptiles – including adders, which are no danger to humans provided they are not approached or disturbed. Tiger beetle and silver-studded blue butterfly survive in this part of the walk with purple hairstreak in the oak woods near the Information Room. This part of the walk is the best place to see and hear woodlark, another species increasing in numbers at Frensham in recent years.

▶ To continue the walk, follow the green markers, climbing the bracken-covered Warren Hill before returning to the side of the Great Pond.

Near Frensham Ponds Hotel, the walk passes the pond outfall, the site of a mill, before joining Pond Lane and continuing around the Pond's south-east corner. Here is another sanctuary and in summer many pairs of reed warbler live in the reed beds. Turning back to the Information Room the route joins the outward walk to the Little Pond (but in reverse). The sandy beaches on the right have been created by erosion, and are a substitute for the seaside for many visitors – this is the most crowded part of the property where wardens are often asked when the tide will be in!

Other walks

The remaining short walks are the Heathland Explorer walk (purple waymarks) and the Easier Access Loop.

The Explorer (touched upon in the course of our walk above) concentrates on the heath and demonstrates how land usage changes; the commons are now managed for wildlife, while the commoners of earlier centuries relied on it to provide thatching and broom-making from heather, with gorse supplying animal fodder and fuel (see article p.108).

As its name implies, the Easier Access Route is particularly intended for wheelchair users and people with pushchairs. In part on a boardwalk across heather, it supplies a 'crash course' in the landscape of the area in the space of 450 yards, passing through several habitats.

WALK 19

WITLEY & MILFORD COMMONS

Map: OS 1:25,000 Explorer 145 Guildford & Farnham

OS grid reference: SU 932405

Distance: 3½ miles

Terrain: Level, mostly unmade paths, can be very wet.

Getting there: By car – A3 (from north follow signs on left; from south go to Elstead/Milford turning back (2 roundabouts) to rejoin A3). Alternative route along A286 Haslemere-Milford road to the Visitor Centre car park

By train – to Milford station

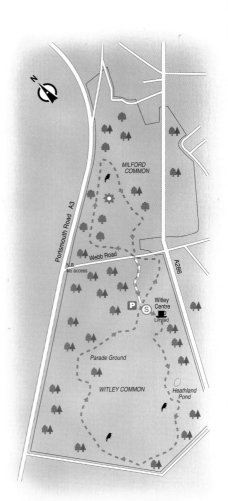

Witley and Milford Commons are adjoining areas of woodland and heath with a wide range of habitats developed as a result of grazing and the military use of the land during the World Wars. The suggested walk is relatively short but it includes parts of both commons, allowing a glimpse of a truly remarkable number of species, flora and fauna; for the naturalist, it almost demands a leisurely approach. The commons do have many paths and a 'do-it-yourself' walk will uncover many other pleasures – a useful leaflet showing bridleway, walk and cycle routes is obtainable from the Information Centre beyond the car park.

Light refreshments are available here, as are WCs.

A circular walk from Witley Centre car park

▶ From the car park follow the red markers (Heathland Hike) past the Centre, through woodland to the wet heath area of the commons.

This is the last trace of the bogs once widespread here. Plants characteristic of this wet heath are cross-leaved heath (with flowers in small, drooping clusters), bog asphodel and bog cotton grass (common together – but seldom in the south-east), sundews and a rich variety of mosses. Just off the route is Heathland Pond, a haven for dragonflies, water boatmen, diving beetles and many other insects.

Surrounding the wet area is dry heath, its many sandy tracks fulfilling several roles, acting as firebreaks and supporting insects like ground-nesting wasps, mining bees and spiders; in warm weather look out for lizards and adders. Ground-feeding tree pipit (summer only) and woodlark – decreasing in recent years but holding on here – join their respective 'cousins' the meadow pipit and skylark. Butterflies begin to appear in the spring, and about 30 species have been noted here – one of the smallest and rarest is the silver-studded blue, feeding on heather between May and August. By late summer bell and common heather cover the dry heath.

▶ The route turns back parallel with the Portsmouth Road (the A3) across a grassy area to enter the wooded areas in which oak is prominent.

The tally of bird species is impressive at any season, while in autumn, fungi – about 400 species – appear in most habitats. The poisonous fly agaric, looking like a fairy toadstool, is found near to silver birch while the deadly death cap favours the oak. Scots pine, some of considerable age, are prominent in the open areas and margins with silver birch and Turkey oak, while hawthorn grows on the margins of the many glades.

Above: A fly agaric – about 400 species of fungi can be found on these commons.

▶ Follow the markers to the right, passing to the north of the Parade Ground; the commons were used as army camps in both World Wars – now they are grazed by long-horned cattle and sheep. To restore the Common after the last war, the impacted surface was broken up and covered with chalky soil from the nearby Hog's Back. The effect was to introduce chalk-loving insects, mosses and flowers but now the chalk is being washed away and they will gradually disappear.

About halfway along the Parade Ground, turn left and follow the yellow marker posts (Soldiers Stroll) to the mixed woodlands, where roe deer may be seen.

🐦 **Redpoll, siskin, coal tit and goldcrest move rapidly, acrobatically in the tree canopy high above the route, calling excitedly – often the best identification of these species.**

▶ The 'stroll' leads to the car park – continue the walk by picking up the orange markers 'Woodlouse Trail' towards the corner of the common, then left to join the entrance drive and cross Webb Road to enter Milford Common. Follow the orange markers in a clock-wise direction, towards the A3.

🌼🐦 **This part of the walk is almost entirely through a mixture of wooded habitat and thorn scrub. Milford soil is naturally more loamy and fertile, attracting bramble, gorse and hawthorn. Polish forces based here in the Second World War planted masses of hawthorn to soften the landscape; the National Trust controls the growth of pine and birch, the great colonisers, allowing the hawthorn to thrive. Gorse is an important food and habitat family – the dense foliage of the spring flowering common gorse provides breeding sites for birds, including the charming stonechat, while its flowers supply pollen to many insect species. It is in the scrub areas of Milford that the nightingale may be heard, competing with the traffic on the A3!**

▶ Follow the markers back to the road and then walk back up the drive to the car park.

Above: A ride through a plantation on Witley Common

Above: Winter on
Witley Common

Right: Heathland
restored after tree
clearance

WALK 20

THE THAMES PATH, CENTRAL LONDON

Maps: OS 1:25,000 Explorer 161 London South & 173 London North

OS grid reference: TQ 332803 (London Bridge Station)

Distance: 7 miles (+ 5 miles, see below)

Terrain: Mostly pavement; some steps, cobbles, grass; footwear that cushions the feet is recommended.

Getting there: By train/Underground – London Bridge Station, or at any convenient train station/Underground

By bus – many local services

By car – not recommended

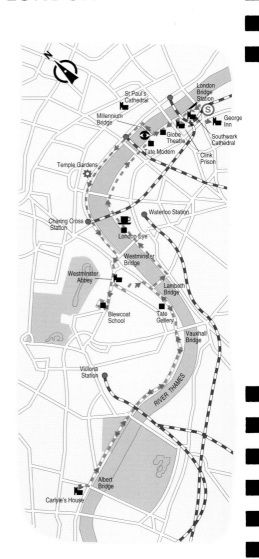

The Thames Path on both sides of the river allows walkers, cyclists and joggers to enjoy London old and new – from the majesty of St Paul's and Southwark Cathedrals, and Westminster Abbey to the London Eye; from Cleopatra's Needle to the Millennium Bridge. A rich variety of historic and modern buildings, gardens, theatres, art galleries, museums, linked by the river, are easily accessible from the route.

The seven-mile walk may be joined at many points and treated as linear or circular. The second, five-mile leg is a return journey from Lambeth Bridge along the northern Thames Path to Chelsea.

The main circular route begins and ends at London Bridge

▶ From London Bridge station, walk left up Duke Street; cross over the bridge's southern end to descend Nancy's Steps, a concealed flight past Bridge House.

The name of these steps commemorates the scene in Dickens' *Oliver Twist*, when Nancy's tragic attempt to save Oliver ended with her murder.

▶ Turn left along a cobbled lane, past the Mudlark pub, and curve left.

Southwark Cathedral, formerly St Mary Overy's Church, was built between 1220 and 1420.

▶ A short detour, for the route leaves the river at this point, leads to an inlet housing a replica of Francis Drake's vessel, the *Golden Hinde*. Retreating from the inlet, go right along Pickford's Wharf into Clink Street.

'The Clink', the prison that gave its name to all the others, was owned by the Bishops of Winchester from the 15th century. From the 12th century until its destruction in 1780, prisoners here ranged from priests to prostitutes. The ruin on the left, with the skeleton of a once superb rose window, is the remains of the one-time palace of the Bishops of Winchester. The next landmark is The Anchor public house, back on the Thames Path.

Walk along Bankside, passing the Globe Theatre and Tate Modern.

Walk across the Millennium Bridge, enjoying views of St Paul's Cathedral, and down steps to rejoin the Thames Path on the north side of the river. Walk westwards under the two Blackfriars bridges, to reach ramped access to Paul's Wharf and steps up to the Embankment.

▶ Continue in a westerly direction along the Embankment, past several moored craft.

A detour to the delightful Temple Gardens on the right is recommended for their tranquillity, and a sense of being anywhere but in central London.

▶ Under Waterloo Bridge, there are views of Big Ben ahead, and the London Eye across the river. Walk under Charing Cross Bridge, past Cleopatra's Needle.

Cleopatra's Needle, erected on this spot in 1879, was actually constructed for Tuthmose III and is carved with hieroglyphics. The history of the obelisk, and those involved in its journey from Egypt, is given on four plaques around its base.

▶ Continue to Westminster Bridge. A detour is worthwhile here, to the National Trust's charming little Blewcoat School. Walk through Parliament Square, along Victoria Street; turn right down Broadway, past New Scotland Yard; take the first left along Caxton Street to the Blewcoat School on the left.

Built in 1709 by a local brewer for the education of the poor, it was in use as a school until 1926. In addition to housing a shop, it is worth a visit for its architectural merit.

Return along Victoria Street, through Westminster Abbey churchyard on the right, pause to admire the Henry Moore sculpture on the green opposite Westminster School, and cross Millbank to rejoin the Thames Path through the Victoria Tower Gardens.

Cross Lambeth Bridge now for the return journey, or continue to Chelsea past Millbank Tower and the Tate Gallery.

Walk across the end of Vauxhall Bridge into Grosvenor Road, past Chelsea Bridge and Cheyne Walk to Chelsea Embankment. At Albert Bridge, turn right down Oakley Street, and left along Cheyne Row to Carlyle's House (NT) at No.24.

Above: The Blewcoat School Shop, Westminster.

Right: The 17th-century George Inn, Southwark, the only remaining galleried inn in London.

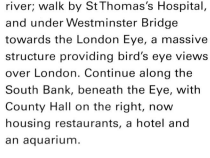

Thomas Carlyle, the 'Sage of Chelsea', lived in this Queen Anne house for some 47 years until his death in 1881. The Victorian décor, furniture and effects are still in place.

▶ Retrace the route to Lambeth Bridge, crossing to the south side, and walking eastwards along the Path. Pass Lambeth Pier, admiring the classic views of the Houses of Parliament and Big Ben across the river; walk by St Thomas's Hospital, and under Westminster Bridge towards the London Eye, a massive structure providing bird's eye views over London. Continue along the South Bank, beneath the Eye, with County Hall on the right, now housing restaurants, a hotel and an aquarium.

Refreshments are available here, and at the many pubs and restaurants along the Path.

▶ Continue under several bridges, to rejoin the outward route at the Millennium Bridge. Walk along St Bedale Street, south of Southwark Cathedral; arrive at the end of London Bridge, turn right and cross Southwark Bridge Road and Borough High Street. A little way along on the right is George Inn Yard with the historic George Inn (NT) – the only remaining galleried inn in London, and very near London Bridge station.

The George Inn was famous as a coaching inn during the 17th century and was mentioned by Dickens in *Little Dorrit*.

Left: Carlyle's House, Chelsea

WALK 21

THE WANDLE TRAIL

Map: OS 1:25,000 Explorer 161 London South

OS Grid reference: TQ 268704 (Colliers Wood Underground)

Distance: 7¹/₂ miles

Terrain: Mostly flat, varied surfaces, including some pavement. Sections can be muddy and uneven, some tree roots, etc. Stout footwear advisable.

Getting there: By train – Colliers Wood Underground; Wimbledon train and Underground (then tram to various points en route)

By bus – local services

By car – A24 between Morden and Tooting

The walk is accessible at many points; the Tramlink system between Wimbledon and Croydon allows it to be sampled in sections.

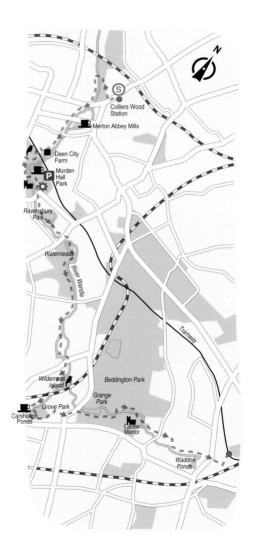

The joy of this walk lies in discovering significant rural stretches and appreciating the industrial history of the River Wandle. Too shallow and fast-flowing for navigation, it proved ideal for milling; it has been claimed that no river of comparable length supported as many mills. Over the centuries changes occurred; the monastic corn-mills progressed to producing dyewood, copper and, finally, paperboard, ceasing production in 1984. Fulling, gun-powder, leather and snuff mills all flourished, briefly, but the development of the steam engine led to a rapid decline. At Merton Abbey Mills the wheel still turns and a few others survive. The Snuff Mill (NT) in Morden Hall Park is well preserved.

A linear walk from Colliers Wood Underground station to Waddon Way Tramlink station

▶ From Colliers Wood Station, cross the High Street into Wandle Meadow Nature Park, containing the little-known Millpond Gardens (NT). Return and re-cross the road, walking past the large supermarket. Turn left, joining the Wandle Trail beside the river; a display panel identifies the site of William Morris's factory (see p.128).

Merton Abbey (in reality an Augustinian Priory) was founded in 1114 and survived to the Dissolution in 1538. It was influential – Thomas à Becket and Adrian IV, the only English Pope, were both educated at the priory; and a seat of power – Henry VI was crowned and lived here. The Statute of Merton in 1235 was the basis of the common law in England, only repealed in 1948. Yet within weeks of the Dissolution, this vast priory was demolished – a few stones remain, close to Merantun Way.

Divert left to Merton Abbey Mills, former site of the Liberty Mills.

Pub; WCs.

▶ Continue along the trail, with the river on the left, through Bunce's Meadow and past Deen City Farm, into Morden Hall Park (NT).

The wetland area experiment here has encouraged visitors like teal and snipe; the rose-ringed parakeet has recently colonised the park, joining regulars like heron, sparrowhawk and woodpecker.

▶ Walking through the park, Morden Hall, home of Nelson's mistress Emma Hamilton, is to the right. Continue to the Snuff Mill and its millrace.

 Beyond are craft shops, and a garden centre/NT shop/restaurant complex. WCs.

▶ Return and walk over a wrought-iron bridge to a lime avenue, turning right through the restored rose garden with its tiny tributary of the river.

The path, fringed by chestnut trees, curves round several ponds with willow, gunnera and many water birds. In winter, there is a chance of seeing a rarity.

▶ On leaving the park, follow signs into Ravensbury Park; walk through to London Road.

 There is a café in the park, and WCs.

▶ Turn right past Watermeads (NT reserve – access only by key, from Morden Hall NT office), and left beyond the reserve. The path returns to the riverbank opposite Bennett's Hole Nature Reserve – the area is rich in plant and birdlife. Beyond Middleton Road, the route passes housing estates before reaching Hackbridge Road. Ignore signs; turn right then left down the Causeway, meeting the trail again in River Gardens, near the entrance to Wilderness Island. Two arms of the River Wandle merge in this nature reserve.

Wholly unexpected, the reserve is well worth visiting – grebe, wagtail and kingfisher are among the regulars.

▶ Follow the waymarked route along Mill Lane and enter Grove Park, with its attractive water features, leading to Carshalton Ponds, ringed by pleasing buildings.

Below: The White Bridge over the river in Morden Hall Park

Divert along Honeywood Walk to the local Heritage Centre for information and tea-rooms.

▶ Return to the park and follow the signs to Beddington Park, where the route criss-crosses the river through pleasant meadowland.

Carew Manor (open) was, for 400 years, the home of the Carew family who introduced and grew oranges at the manor as early as 1580. An attractive grouping is completed by the 14th-century church and some cottages.

▶ Continue east over Beddington Lane, and the river flows past several delightful weather-boarded mill cottages. Facing them is Lambert's Mill, once a snuff mill. Follow signs past Richmond Green and along a bridlepath. The Wandle disappears beneath an industrial estate and the Trail ends at Waddon Ponds, a source of the river.

Walk on, crossing Waddon Way, to Vicarage Road, some 400 yards. From here take the Tramlink system into Croydon, or back to Wimbledon.

Below: Willow and waterfall, Morden Hall Park

Right: Autumn in the Avenue at Morden Hall Park

FAMOUS FIGURES IN THE LANDSCAPE

If King John had hoped to appease his nobles by meeting them at Runnymede on 15 June 1215, he was quickly disabused of the idea, accepting the strength of their position, and his own weakness. Essentially a feudal document, the Magna Carta included concessions to the agricultural and commercial classes. Amongst these was reform of the forest law; the famous clause 39 stated that a freeman should not

Above: Flatford Mill

be punished unless by the lawful judgment of his peers and by the law of the land. This became the basis of the modern constitution.

In the late 1950s the Magna Carta Trust, supported by the American Bar Association, commissioned a memorial to Magna Carta, which stands on Cooper's Hill overlooking the meadows at Runnymede. Later,

Above: Sandham Memorial Chapel

the American Bar Association provided a memorial to President John F. Kennedy, standing close to the earlier one, on an acre of ground given to the American people by the people of Britain.

John Constable and Stanley Spencer may differ dramatically in style, but devotion to the countryside illuminates their work. Constable's birthplace was East Bergholt; he walked to school in Dedham through the Dedham Vale beside the River Stour, the subject of many of his paintings. Flatford Mill and Willy Lott's Cottage were major subjects; they are relatively unchanged today.

More than a century later, in 1891, Stanley Spencer was born in Cookham, where he remained for much of his life. An individualist, he painted hundreds of scenes, many of biblical events depicted as if they had taken place in the village. His war

Above: Bronze statue of Carlyle

scenes, particularly the murals on the walls of Sandham Memorial Chapel (NT) at Burghclere, near Newbury, are both powerful and moving.

Industrialisation during the Victorian era promoted mass production of furniture, cloth and ornamental objects. William Morris, poet, artist and architect, rejected this, favouring instead simplicity, craftsmanship and good design – and this marked the beginning of the Arts and Crafts Movement. Morris moved his factory to Merton Abbey in 1881, and the firm occupied the site until 1940, engaged in weaving, dyeing, block printing and producing stained glass. There is a small commemorative museum at the Merton Abbey Mills site.

Naturally, Knole is rich with historical figures, from Queen Elizabeth I to the 20th-century writer and gardener, Vita Sackville-West, who grew up in the house. The house is home to the Sackville family. Thomas, the 1st Earl, wrote the first drama in English; Charles Sackville, the rakish 6th Earl, took Nell Gwynn as his mistress and entertained his literary friends in Poets' Parlour.

The Scottish historian, essayist and sociological writer, Thomas Carlyle, moved from Scotland with his wife Jane in 1834, to the Queen Anne house in Chelsea, now called Carlyle's House. Jane, whose own correspondence is now accepted as outstanding, died in 1866; Thomas remained in the house until his death in 1881.

When he was not at Westminster, Winston Churchill's home, and his great joy, was the Kentish manor house of Chartwell, where he and his wife lived from 1924 until his death in 1965. Churchill created much of the garden including the lakes; his garden studio contains many of his paintings. The house is largely unaltered since his death.

Above: Churchill lived at Chartwell from 1924 until his death.

WALK 22

HAMPSTEAD AND THE HEATH

Map: OS 1:25,000 Explorer 173: London North

OS grid reference: TQ 263858 (Hampstead Underground station)

Distance: 5 miles

Terrain: Mostly hardened paths with a variety of surfaces from pavement to earth. Some steeper slopes, but otherwise gentle gradients.

Getting there: By train – Hampstead Heath Station, 1 mile from Fenton House, ½ mile from 2 Willow Road

Underground – Hampstead

By bus – frequent local services

By car – park at Jack Straw's Castle public house, at Kenwood, and near Willow Road, Hampstead.

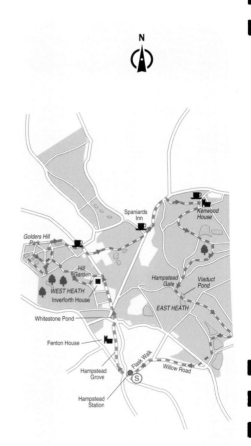

There is much to explore on the Heath, including nearby areas such as Highgate Ponds and Parliament Hill Fields. The suggested route passes three historic houses, and a variety of gardens, all open to the public. There are no waymarks as such, but an excellent map, covering the area of the walk, is obtainable from The Corporation of London for a small fee (tel. 020 7485 4491).

A circular walk from Hampstead Underground station

▶ Cross Heath Street, and walk up Holly Hill; fork right into Hampstead Grove – Fenton House (NT), is on the left.

🏠 **Fenton House, late 17th century, contains a fine collection of early keyboard instruments. Much of the delightful, secluded walled garden probably dates from the same William and Mary period.**

▶ Continue up Hampstead Grove to the edge of the Heath at Whitestone Pond; walk over West Heath Road, by the pond's eastern edge, and along North End Way, passing the well-known pub, Jack Straw's Castle, on the left.

A little further on, beyond Inverforth House, turn left into Inverforth Close, a gated road which forks in about 50 yards. The left-hand fork passes beneath a Georgian pergola forming a bridge linking Inverforth House and the Hill Garden. The pergola contains a variety of scented plants and is reached via a spiral staircase. The Hill Garden, in sharp contrast, is more formal, but equally enjoyable. Continue through the wooded West Heath, taking the path leading west, away from the Hill Garden. Cross

Below: Kenwood House, Hampstead

Sandy Road to reach Golders Hill Park, with its animal enclosures and aviary. Walk past the deer enclosure, turning left on a short detour to see the other animals and birds, and visit the Water Garden. Return and turn north, passing the hill and bandstand. Forward towards the lily pond, crossing over a small humpbacked bridge, to explore the garden, with its arbours and pool. Continue eastwards, past the refreshment building.

Leaving the park, turn right along North End Road. In a few yards, cross at the Bull and Bush public house on the left and walk along North End Avenue, through the gate at the end, and onto the wooded heath at Sandy Road. Go forward for

Above: Fallow deer at Golders Hill Park

about a third of a mile, with ponds on the right, to Heath End on Spaniards Road. Cross the road, turning left past the 16th-century Spaniards Inn.

After some 350 yards, enter Kenwood at West Lodge, on the right. Walk on a short distance to the neo-classical house, built in the 17th century and remodelled by Adam, with its outstanding collection of paintings.

Refreshments are available in the Stables Restaurant.

▶ On the south side of the house, turn right along the Lime Walk, enjoying the views downhill; note the Henry Moore sculpture on the left. Follow the curve of the path downhill, glancing back at the superb views of the house. Cross Stone Bridge over Wood Pond, taking the second right-hand turning, level with the Open Air Stage area on the left.

This path through Ken Wood, which is a fine bluebell wood in spring, continues past the Duelling Ground on the right before meeting a T-junction. Turn right, taking the next left fork, and continue along a 350-yard stretch (likely to be muddy in wet weather) and along a path lined with low paling fences. This is joined by another path on the right, at the end of the Kenwood Estate, and leads through the gate and on for a few yards through an opening in a fence, until it meets a junction of several paths at Hampstead Gate. There are seats here in a clearing; continue through a more open piece of ground, before crossing over Bird Bridge.

Turn left along Viaduct Avenue, passing across Viaduct Pond, once swampy ground, over which the Viaduct was built in the mid-19th century. Continue along the Avenue for some 400 yards before passing between the Mixed Bathing and Hampstead No.2 Ponds. The Avenue turns right past the fairground site and a large public car park on the right.

The central house of a terrace of three, 2 Willow Road was designed and built in 1939 by Ernö Goldfinger, the leading Modernist architect. It contains his art collection and furniture he designed for the house.

Go forward into Downshire Hill opposite, turning first right, and you'll reach 2 Willow Road (NT) immediately on the left.

▶ Complete the walk along two of the most attractive streets in Hampstead Village. Continue up Willow Road, a steep climb, before turning along Flask Walk. At Heath Street, the Underground station is on the right.

Above: A glade on Hampstead Heath

Above: Flask Walk, Hampstead

WALK 23

HAWKWOOD & PETTS WOOD

Map: OS 1:25,000 Explorer 162 Greenwich & Gravesend

OS grid reference: TQ 440679

Distance: 4 miles

Terrain: Mostly flat, some climbs. Much of this walk is not suitable for people with mobility impairment, due to several footbridges, tree roots and other uneven surfaces. Stout shoes advisable, particularly after wet weather.

Getting there: By train – Petts Wood station

By bus – various local services

By car – 1½ miles off A21 at Bromley Common, ½ mile off A208 Chislehurst/Orpington Road

This walk is accessible at several points – Petts Wood Station, Tent Peg Lane car park and Thornet Wood car park.

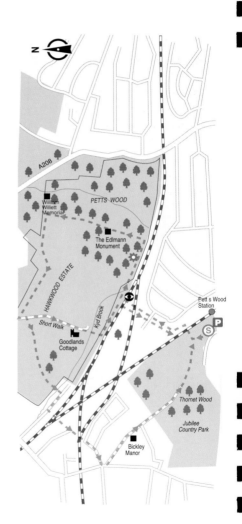

To find a walk of some four miles through woodland and farmland, in the middle of a heavily populated area on the London/North Kent border, may seem improbable. This walk achieves that and, were it not for the sound of trains – including Eurostar – travelling to and from London, the walker might be in the depths of the country.

A circular walk from Tent Peg Lane car park

The walk is one of an excellent series developed by Bromley Countryside Ranger Service. The early part is also along a section of the London Loop – the London Outer Orbital Path.

▶ The walk begins at Tent Peg Lane car park (no charge), close to Petts Wood Station, on the edge of Jubilee Country Park. Established in 1978 to commemorate the Queen's Silver Jubilee, the park is now a designated local Nature Reserve. Starting in woodland – silver birch, aspen, oak, bramble and wild rose – which has developed since the 1970s, when the area ceased to be allotments, the walk soon reaches the first of three railway bridges.

Behind some houses, the path crosses a cul de sac, Little Thrift, then two more railway bridges, the last giving superb views of the Petts Wood and Hawkwood Estates (NT).

Only a few farm buildings disturb the panorama of sloping fields and woodland.

▶ Turn right beside the railway, and shortly the walk crosses the Kyd Brook. Continue, briefly, beside the river and, on reaching Petts Wood, take the lower path, closest to the railway.

Below: A view over sloping fields and woodland

135

❈ This section of path may be narrow and overgrown in late summer with rosebay willowherb, bramble and nettle predominating. Boardwalks have been laid over areas inclined to become boggy in wet weather.

▶ The path forks again after a short distance, and the left-hand path up the hill goes through a damp area with pendulous sedge. In about 400 yards, the path drops down to a National Trust information panel. Turn sharp left and take either the footpath or the parallel bridleway, a slightly easier surface. The route climbs gently up between two woods.

🌳 Mature birch and standard pay homage to Francis Edlmann, who saved the wood on the left in 1927, and William Willett, founder of British Summer Time. The Edlmann Monument is in a small clearing on the left, 200 yards up the path.

Above: The path passes grazing animals

▶ Soon, the view to the left opens out at a field, named Soldiering Field for the military volunteers who were drilled here in the 19th century. At the end of the field, on the edge of St Paul's Cray Common, our route turns left, leaving the London Loop. Make a short detour on, and to the right, visiting the memorial stone commemorating William Willett. Return to the field edge and turn along its northern boundary.

The narrow and uneven path continues downhill, passing the tree-rimmed Flusher's Pond on the right; boardwalks cover a particularly muddy area. Continue by climbing gently through woodland, then on the ridge near Coopers' School fields; there are more fine views to the left over the Hawkwood Estate.

Before continuing with the full walk, take another short detour down the metalled Botany Bay Lane to see Goodlands Cottage, beside Hawkwood Farm.

🏰 Goodlands Cottage is a 17th-century Grade 2 listed building, built of red brick, with charming arched windows.

▶ Return uphill and turn left onto a pleasant path, passing beside fields with grazing animals, before dropping down into a valley with a wood on the left. Here is another pastoral scene, somewhat difficult to reconcile with the railway hidden below and with Bickley and Bromley encroaching just beyond the skyline – the spire across the valley belongs to St George's, Bickley.

Cross over the Kyd Brook, continuing to the end of the path, turning right into Gosshill Road, and left under a bridge (the least attractive part of the walk) into Barfield Road. Walk to Blackbrook Lane, and immediately turn left into Thornet Wood Road. Pass Bickley Manor on the right (rather more Cheshire than Kent in terms of architectural style) and at Bromley High School the road becomes single track.

Walk on past the car park on the right at the edge of Thornet Wood. Now the track is a shared pedestrian and cycle route across oak and hazel coppice, with meadows managed for their wild flowers. Turn right at the kissing gates and return to Tent Peg Lane car park.

▶ For a shorter walk (total about 3 miles), turn left at Botany Bay Lane, passing the farm and cottage buildings, dropping down through open fields to cross once more over the Kyd Brook. Turn left to rejoin the outward route by the third railway bridge and return to the car park.

Below: The route climbs gently through woodland

WALK 24

DUNSTABLE AND WHIPSNADE DOWNS

Map: OS 1:25,000 Explorer 181 & 182

OS grid reference: TL008198 (Countryside Centre – not NT)

Distance: 2½ miles; 4½ miles

Terrain: Varied, quite hilly around Dunstable Downs. Can be muddy and uneven in places. Stout footwear required at all seasons.

Getting there: By car – At W end of Dunstable, between B4540 & B4541 nearby By bus – Luton/Hemel Hempstead

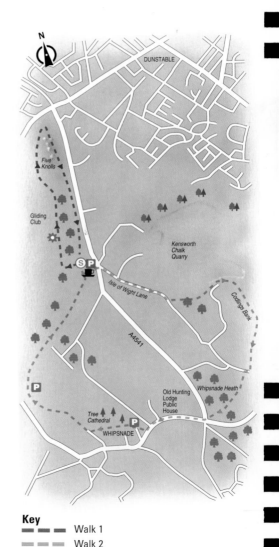

The walks have the advantage of being accessible at several points: Dunstable Downs, Bison Hill, Whipsnade Tree Cathedral and Whipsnade Crossroads, with car-parking at each point.

Of the many attractive walks in this area we have selected two, both beginning at the Dunstable Downs Countryside Centre (NT). The parking area is ideal for people to take in the marvellous views over the Vale of Aylesbury. There are leaflets (produced by Bedfordshire County Council) describing various designated circular routes on the Downs; we have amalgamated parts of them in our walks, believing these may be somewhat easier-going than the

Key

▬ ▬ ▬ Walk 1

▬ ▬ ▬ Walk 2

designated walks, two of which involve a steepish climb at the end.

 Refreshments and WCs are available at the Centre.

Two circular walks from Dunstable Downs Countryside Centre

Walk 1

We suggest taking the shorter (2¹/₂ miles) walk first.

▶ From the Centre, walk down the hill in a southwesterly direction towards the airfield, and be entertained en route by gliders, light aircraft and small boys flying kites on this spectacular chalk scarp. The well-trodden sunken chalk and flint path (steep and rutted, care needed) curves to the right at the foot of the hill and skirts the airfield along a nettle and cow parsley-fringed bridlepath through hawthorn, wild roses and honeysuckle, and the inevitable elderberry. On weekdays, the route can be surprisingly unfrequented.

Away from the shrub canopy, with noisy crows wheeling above, continue through more open land at the foot of the scarp.

Below: The spectacular chalk scarp, Dunstable Downs

Poppies, wild roses and white campion are just a few of many wild flowers to be seen here in early summer.

▶ Walk straight on at the point where the bridlepath turns left along the strangely named Worthington-Smith Lane, giving access to an alternative walk (see p.142); note the path runs along a terrace, almost certainly part of a medieval type of cultivation called a strip lynchet.

The bridlepath left behind, walk on along the gently rising path, leading past the Bronze Age burial mounds of Five Knolls on the hill to the right (it is possible to cut off a corner here and climb up the steep escarpment). The path passes the backs of some gardens before emerging onto an open space on the extreme edge of Dunstable. Turn sharp right, climbing to the top of the escarpment, and walk along the beautifully grassy path, cropped by sheep for part of the year, back to the Countryside Centre. Your eyes will be drawn constantly to the memorable views.

Below: A view over the Vale of Aylesbury

Right: Whipsnade Tree Cathedral: the nave, looking east

Walk 2

▶ Starting again from the Centre, cross the B4541, taking the left-hand fork, Isle of Wight Lane (heavy traffic, take care). Near the radio masts, pass Greenacres, turning left beside an arable field, along the edge of Kensworth Chalk Quarry, an SSSI, then onwards through a tree plantation. The footpath turns south, uphill past Codlings Bank, then forward to Greenend Farm, where it turns briefly right onto Isle of Wight Lane before left across fields to the common land of Whipsnade Heath.

At Whipsnade crossroads, walk along the road past the Old Hunting Lodge Public House, following the signs to the Tree Cathedral (NT) at the edge of the village green.

This unique planting of trees, in the form of a medieval cathedral, was created in 'faith, hope and reconciliation' by Edmund Kell Blyth to commemorate two of his close friends killed at the end of the First World War. Grass avenues form chancel, nave, transepts, chapels and cloisters. There is also a dew pond.

▶ From here the waymarked route skirts some fields before turning sharp right along a lane (can be wet at the end) past the Wild Animal Park car park. The lane, probably the old route linking Whipsnade with Eaton Bray, leads to Eaton Bray Common and the NT's Bison Hill car park with its fine views. From here, follow the bridleway downhill for a short distance before turning right and walking across fields and scrub on the top of the scarp – more fine views – to the Centre.

USEFUL CONTACTS

The National Trust
Further details and opening arrangements of all NT properties can be found in the current National Trust Handbook, the National Trust Coast & Countryside Handbook, or on our website www.nationaltrust.org.uk

You can also buy National Trust books from this site.

If you would like to join, please write to:

The National Trust Membership Department
PO Box 39
Bromley
Kent
BR1 3XL

The Clink Prison Museum
Website: www.clink.co.uk

The Corporation of London
Tel. 020 7485 4491

English Heritage
Customer Services
PO Box 569
Swindon
SN2 2YP
Tel. 01793 414910
Email: customers@english-heritage.org.uk

Membership enquries
PO Box 570
Swindon
SN2 2UR
Email: members@english-heritage.org.uk

Flatford
NT tel. 01206 298260

Field Studies Council,
Flatford Mill
Tel. 01206 298283

Sir Alfred Munnings Art Museum
Tel. 01206 322127

Flatford TIC
Tel. 01206 299460

Bridge Cottage, Constable exhibition and guided walks
Tel. 01206 298260

Kenwood House (English Heritage)
Hampstead, London
Tel. 020 8348 1286

London LOOP
The London Outer Orbital Path is a 150-mile route around London. Details available from the London Walking Forum.
Tel. 020 7247 3564

Museum of Garden History
Tel. 020 7401 8865
Email: info@museumgardenhistory.org
Website www.museumgardenhistory.org

Northey Island (NT)
Resident warden
Tel. 01621 853142

The Royal Botanic Gardens, Kew
Website: www.rbgkew.org.uk

The Stanley Spencer Gallery, Cookham
Tel. 01628 471885
Website www.stanleyspencer.org

Syon Park
Brentford, Middlesex TW8 8JF
Tel. 020 8560 0883

PHOTO CREDITS